Henry Howson, Charles Howson

A Brief Inquiry into the Principles, Effect, and Present State of the American Patent System

Henry Howson, Charles Howson

A Brief Inquiry into the Principles, Effect, and Present State of the American Patent System

ISBN/EAN: 9783337311780

Printed in Europe, USA, Canada, Australia, Japan

Cover: Foto ©Suzi / pixelio.de

More available books at **www.hansebooks.com**

A BRIEF INQUIRY

INTO THE

PRINCIPLES, EFFECT, AND PRESENT STATE

OF THE

AMERICAN PATENT SYSTEM

BY

H. & C. HOWSON.

TOGETHER WITH THE

Laws of the United States Relating to Patents, Trade-Marks and Copyrights.

PHILADELPHIA:
SHERMAN & CO., PRINTERS.
1872.

Entered according to Act of Congress, in the year 1871,

By H. & C. HOWSON,

In the Office of the Librarian of Congress at Washington, D. C.

CONTENTS.

	PAGE
Preface,	3
History of property in inventions,	5
General principles governing patent property,	9
Patents as a mode of remunerating inventors,	12
Essential features of a good patent system,	15
The American patent system.—Previous official examination,	17
Ordinary criticisms of the Patent Office considered,	24
Actual defects of the Patent Office and the remedy,	28
Benefits of an examining system,	34
The examining system as viewed from abroad,	37
Remedies for defective patents,	46
Disclaimers—Reissues,	50
General features of the U. S. Patent Laws,	56
Caveats,	57
Conditions to patentability,	58
Interferences,	61
Priority of invention,	65
Diligence,	67
Appeals,	68
Remedies for Infringement,	69
Laws of the United States relating to patents, trade marks and copyrights,	73
Index to patent laws,	109

PREFACE.

The following brief essay on the Patent System of the United States contains information which the writers believe has not heretofore been collected in a treatise of reasonable compass. To obtain such information inventors have been compelled to resort for some items to the Patent Laws, for others to the Rules and Regulations of the Patent Office; while others of great importance have been, to all practical intents, locked up in elaborate volumes to which none but a professional man could be expected to give the requisite time and attention.

The aim in the following pages has been, in part, to collect and condense information concerning the general features of the law, illustrating it, where necessary, by reference to general principles.

In doing this it has been pertinent to enter at some length into those questions of public justice and policy upon which property in invention is founded, and to explain the true position of inventors in relation to the public.

Official examination, previous to the grant of patents, has been treated at some length, and necessarily in a controversial way, the endeavor being to meet, in a fair and scrutinizing spirit, the usual objections to the system, to point out wherein it may be really deficient, and how capable of remedy these deficiencies are.

We believe that the question is fairly stated, and candidly considered, and we trust that our readers will conclude with us that whatever may have been the defects in the examining system, they are susceptible of remedy, and that all defects admitted, the system may yet be regarded as one of the most efficient of those causes which have given patent property, here, a certainty and commercial value, such as it possesses in no other patent-granting country.

It is proper to state that our remarks upon the main defect, want of uniformity, in the examining system, and our suggestions as to the remedy are for the most part based upon observations made by the Hon. M. D. Leggett, the present able Commissioner of Patents, who, while keenly alive to the defect alluded to, is not in the least doubtful of the feasibility of measures by which it may be remedied.

To the facts and arguments adduced in support of the examining system additional point is given, by reference to foreign testimony as to the evils arising from the grant of patents without previous examination. It was considered pertinent to do this, because, recently, it has been hinted in sundry quarters that the abandonment of previous examinations would be a desirable improvement in our law. That such a change would be anything but desirable we think our readers can hardly fail to conclude, when they peruse the weighty evidence collected in these pages against a haphazard, undiscriminating grant of patents.

The concluding chapters of the treatise touch upon other leading features in our patent law. Disclaimers, reissues, caveats, interferences, suits for infringement, &c., are treated of, necessarily, with great brevity, but not too briefly, it is hoped, to convey that rudimentary knowledge of the subject which every person interested in patent property should acquire.

Anything like the thoroughness of a legal text-book is, of course, not to be expected within so brief a compass, and in fact anything beyond generalization has been carefully avoided, the object being simply to map out those common principles and incidents which are of everyday application in dealing with property in original invention.

In the book is incorporated the text of the law concerning patents, trade-marks, and copyrights; those sections of the law bearing upon questions treated in the body of the book being there referred to by number.

It is hoped that inventors and patentees will find the treatise a serviceable manual of information touching matters greatly concerning their interests.

H. & C. HOWSON.

THE AMERICAN PATENT SYSTEM.

CHAPTER I.

HISTORY OF PROPERTY IN INVENTIONS.

AN inquiry as to the principles and object of the American Patent System, may perhaps be made more clear if introduced by a brief historical retrospect.

The English "Statute of Monopolies," James I, 21st, is the earliest legislative recognition of the public policy of allowing temporary exclusive rights in the exercise of *new* manufactures. This statute declared utterly illegal and void, those royal grants for the sole buying, selling, working or using of different things within the realm, which, under the name of patents, had become odious from their mischievous and oppressive results. But from the general condemnation of monopolies, the act excepted, under certain qualifications, patents for the sole working or making, during a limited period, of any manner of NEW manufactures, which others, *at the time of making such letters-patent should not use.*

To the Anglo-Saxon mind—jealous of anything tending to restrain free action, and jealous, especially, of any extraordinary instruments of taxation—monopolies in trade or art, or in the making or vending of necessary or useful articles, were utterly abhorrent.

But the *declaratory* character of this statute shows that previously, at common law, it was recognized as a lawful prerogative of the Crown to grant to the inventors of *new* manufactures the sole right, for limited periods, of working such manufactures within the kingdom, and records of such grants are to be found, dating so far back as the time of Edward III.

As explained by Lord Eldon, this was a prerogative vested in the Crown as the depositary of the supreme executive power of the state, to be exercised in behalf of *and for the benefit of the public.*

But, as may be well understood, a royal prerogative of granting Patents of Monopolies, so long as its *true* object remained undefined and its exercise unregulated by express legislation, was exceedingly likely to be diverted from its legitimate uses and employed for the private advantage of the monarch, or of royal favorites, to the *grievous disadvantage* of the public. And so events proved, for during the reign of Elizabeth especially the prerogative was so stretched and perverted as to produce general mischief and complaint, which finally led to the passage of this Statute of Monopolies, the effect of which is to define the *real* extent and object of the royal prerogative with reference to the grant of patents affecting the exercise of trades.

It is not our purpose to pursue this historical inquiry further than to point out that the common law of England early recognized the *public policy* of granting exclusive privileges in the exercise of *new* trades, and that the *public* advantage arising from the introduction or discovery of a new art or trade was regarded as being that which alone warranted such grants.

The words "true and first inventor," as used to this day in English Patent law, include not only him who may first devise or discover something new, but him also who may first make known within the kingdom something which has been invented abroad.

The reason of this is readily understood when we consider the character of the times in which the English law on this subject may first be traced. The insular position of England and the imperfect, not to say dangerous character of travel, isolated her from the rest of the civilized world. Communication was limited and infrequent, and in every country patriotism took the shape of extreme jealousy of foreigners. It is not hard to believe, then, that to import knowledge of an art from abroad was no small achievement, but might be regarded as rare merit.

Thus in the Clothmakers of Ipswich case, adjudged in the reign of James I, it is said, "If a man hath brought in a new invention and a new trade within the kingdom, *in peril of his life and consumption of his estate or stock, &c.*, or if a man hath made a new discovery of anything, in such cases the King, of his grace and favor, in recompense of his cost and travail, may grant by charter unto him that he, only, shall use such a trade or traffique for a certain time, &c."

To the development of invention in the sense of originating and devising, neither the intellectual nor the social condition of these early times was favorable.

The mass of laborers and artisans were little more than human machines, running in one rut, and as a rule lacking the desire or the intelligence to seek to better their modes and means of working, while the intellectual efforts of those of higher rank and educated intelligence were not as yet fairly diverted from the unprofitable channels and mysterious lore of a false and unprofitable philosophy. Bacon's works were but now startling the educated few, and the leaven of that practical and humane philosophy of which he was the first great exponent had yet to commence its work on men's minds. The science of the times was perfectly barren. The artisans were not thinkers, and the thinkers had no acquaintance with the practical arts. There was yet a gulf, partly of social and political and partly of educational creation, separating cultured intelligence and practical industry, which must be allied before there can be fruitful invention.

Nor were the political troubles of the time, succeeded as they shortly were by internal war, favorable to the development of the industrial arts. Moreover the science of physics was yet to be reduced to rational principles, and new modes of thought to be developed, and this was the slow work of years. The application of science to the practical arts must come later.

It is not to be wondered at then, that, as is observed in the excellent treatise of Hindmarch, "for many years after the passing of the statute of monopolies the arts and manufactures continued in a low state in England; few of the inventions for which letters-patent were obtained were of any value, and the demand for novelties being very limited, no one was tempted to infringe the rights of patentees."

It is not until the reign of George III that we find the subject of property in inventions attracting public attention. Then the troubles of Arkwright and of Watt, brought the subject of patents into court, and led to the earliest of that series of judicial reasonings upon the English law of patents, which gives that law what it has of system.

We need not wonder that the early treatment of patents in the English courts was anything but liberal. The subject was a strange one, coming before them at a time when a very clear and high conception of the importance and merit of inventors could hardly exist.

In later years, as the exercise of the inventive faculties became more general and active, and had produced results which forced a perception of the importance and value of original invention upon the public mind, a more liberal treatment of patents crept into the judicial practice; and the English patent law as it stands to-day is for the most part judge-made law, whose doctrines are founded upon reasoning as just and liberal, perhaps, as the bounds of the old legislation forming the text for the judicial commentaries will permit.

The apparent public policy of encouraging improvements in the useful arts, has led to the adoption by most civilized countries of patent systems more or less analogous to that of England.

The earliest to adopt such systems were France and the United States.

Our own patent system, first established by Act of Congress, in 1790, and gradually developed and improved by subsequent legislation, is based upon reasoning which seems, on the whole, peculiarly correct, just, and liberal.

It originated at a time and under circumstances favorable to the development of inventive activity, and which allowed a clear perception of the importance of invention to the domestic progress of the useful arts and its consequent utility to society.

This led to a recognition of the principle of *private right* which really underlies a patent system, and of the broad difference between patent privileges and monopolies, so called.

A monopoly in its legal and odious sense, implies the taking away of some right from the many, for the benefit of particular individuals. Manifestly, then, the term is not applicable to letters-patent for new inventions; that cannot be taken from the public, which the public has not; a new invention or discovery can become public property, only by communication from the inventor or discoverer; until so communicated voluntarily, it remains the secret property of the latter.

This view of the case shows that into the public policy of patents enter important considerations of public justice, an idea upon which we shall have occasion to dwell more fully in the course of this treatise.

Looking to the question how far our patent system may be adjudged from *experience* to have proved consistent with the principles of justice and policy upon which it is based, we find, to begin with, that the number of patents issued in this country, is very largely in excess of that in any other patent-granting country; that there is here a more general and widely-spread inventive activity than elsewhere; that American labor-saving machinery and devices are in demand the world over; and that inventors enjoy in this community, a power and consideration without parallel abroad.

The vast amount of work to be done in developing the resources and industries of this new country, by a comparatively small and scattered population, with moderate pecuniary resources, has made labor-saving mechanism a peculiarly serviceable instrument of power, supplying the place of manual labor with greater accuracy and economy, and so increasing the productive power of capital.

Thus, it is because of its peculiarly manifest utility to the public, that invention has here attained such dignity.

How far has this been brought about by our patent system? or in other words, how far has that system tended to incite and foster the exercise of ingenuity?

Our Patent Laws are, undoubtedly, the most truly liberal of any. They more clearly than any other recognize the truths that productive industry is the basis of national wealth and power; that such industry will flourish in proportion as it is made a *secure* source of individual profit; that true invention is intellectual production of the most beneficial kind, and that, therefore, true policy, which is always just, demands that it shall be made, as far as posssible, a secure source of individual profit.

The benefit of the patent laws has been sought with avidity, and there can be no doubt that the advantages which they hold out have led to a multitude of inventions and novel disclosures, which otherwise had not been made.

But many complaints and criticisms have been directed against the patent laws and their administration (some of them more or less just, no doubt, since an absolutely perfect system of human designing is hardly to be looked for), but for the most part we think fallacious and arising from a misapprehension of the true principles of the law.

This misapprehension, it is believed, is to be traced in great degree to the just favor and consideration with which inventors have been regarded, leading gradually to a somewhat one-sided and partial understanding of the laws affecting them.

CHAPTER II.

GENERAL PRINCIPLES GOVERNING PROPERTY IN INVENTIONS.

It is our purpose in this chapter to inquire first into the true nature and purpose of patent laws, for it is necessary to ascertain this, before we can look with intelligence into the question of the justice and efficiency of our own law.

The patent laws, as viewed in reference to inventors only, are the means of securing temporary exclusive rights to the use of new and useful inventions, and it is not unnatural that inventors themselves should regard the laws in that light only. So viewing them, regarding themselves as the only parties interested, they will look with impatience and disfavor upon those features in the laws, or the administration of them, which may seem mere embarrassments or impediments in the way of obtaining patents.

Yet this is not a true, because only a partial, view of the subject.

It would be an unprofitable and unnecessary task to touch upon the question of man's *natural* property in his own original ideas. It is sufficient to recognize the fact that as long as they are locked up in his own breast, they are likely to be of little benefit to himself or any one else; to be of use they must, as a rule, be disclosed; and when once disclosed, they cannot be stamped with the character of individual property, and be identified and protected as such, except through the medium of positive legislation.

But society can be looked to for such legislation only if, and so far as it may be, consistent with the general welfare.

Consequently it is in *utility to society* that we must seek the reason and justification of positive laws recognizing individual rights in connection with invention.

The progress of the useful arts is a most important branch of the general welfare, and inventors are the chief instruments for the advancement of the useful arts. An inventor is not bound to disclose his invention; he may, if he so elect, keep the knowledge of it to himself, but *generally* he cannot himself profit by its use, without, in the very act, disclosing it to others, and when thus disclosed, there is nothing in the absence of positive law on the subject to prevent other members of the public from availing themselves of an idea, which has then in a certain sense become public property.

Evidently, in a state of society where for an inventor to disclose his invention is altogether to lose, without return, the special benefit of it, and of the labor and expense he may have bestowed upon it, there is little or no encouragement for the exercise of ingenuity, and the expenditure of thought, time, labor, and money in the bringing to light of new inventions. Men will not willingly sow merely for others to reap.

It may be said that the inventor derives a profit from his original thought, in the advantage which it gives him over competitors, by way of increased facilities or economy in the prosecution of his business. But if he cannot hope to maintain this power longer than he can keep it secret, but must upon accidental disclosure share his advantage with all his competitors, so that he will then occupy no better position relatively than before, plainly the inducement to invention is small indeed.

It is to be considered, moreover, that in an active condition of the inventive mind, a vast number of original ideas must be produced, which have no relation to the particular employment of the inventors, and for the encouragement of such a general active condition, therefore, some special inducement must exist.

Some few inventions there are which may be practiced in secret, and no doubt valuable and important discoveries have in this way died with their originators, and so been lost to the world. Of such concealment it is desirable that there should be as little as possible, not only because it tends to deprive the public of useful knowledge, but because it tends to destroy confidence, and arouse doubt and suspicion, hampering business, and interfering with peace and good order. The concealment of inventions, where it may appear practicable, will, perhaps, always be to some extent indulged in, but it is evidently impolicy on the part of the public to *encourage* such concealment, by totally ignoring the interests of inventors.

The mischiefs, public and private, likely to proceed from compelling inventors to secrecy, have been thus forcibly represented by an accomplished writer:

" A manufacture conducted in secret, is at an enormous disadvantage. Processes must be separated, that the workman may not apprehend the mystery; immense wages must be paid to retain them from deserting to competitors; simplicity must be avoided, and expense introduced, for no purpose but to complicate and confuse the methods used. Experiments for further improvement must be avoided, for they would not only tend to disclosure, but to the loss of the outlay incurred in establishing the existing expensive methods. After all, if the attempt to maintain the secret were successful, the public would be no gainers, for it would constitute a strict monopoly, and, unlike a patent, a monopoly that would be lasting either till the secret was discovered, or till it died with its first employers."

To this it need only be added that in such a state of affairs, many important improvements would be forever lost, from the inability of the inventors to undertake the burden of practicing them secretly, and their natural unwillingness to run the risks of disclosing them to persons who might assume that burden.

The relative positions then, of the public and inventors, and the consequences proceeding therefrom, may be thus summarized:

I. The public is vitally interested in the progress of the useful arts, and to this progress the production and disclosure of original invention are essential: it is the clearest *public policy* to encourage such production and disclosure by any proper means.

II. Inventors, in producing and disclosing improvements in the useful arts, add materially to the public stock of wealth and power, and are therefore producers of the highest order; and as payment is the rightful consequence of physical or mental labor, time, and capital expended in production, it would seem the clearest *public justice* that some mode should be provided of remunerating inventors in proportion to the value of their productions and disclosures.

III. From the preceding propositions it follows that the public object of promoting the progress of the useful arts is that which allies the interests of the public and those of inventors. The consideration which passes from the inventor to the public, *entitling* him to some return, is his contribution to that progress.

We come then to the conclusions that, practically speaking, the rights of inventors, as such, are those created by positive legislation; and that the object of legislation, in creating such rights, is to promote the progress of the useful arts by providing some mode by which inventors may be remunerated for their instrumentality in promoting that progress.

Thus we find the true object of our own patent system in the title of the original act of 1790, and of the succeeding acts: "An Act to promote the progress of the useful arts."

CHAPTER III.

OF PATENTS AS A MODE OF REMUNERATING INVENTORS.

THE propositions admitted, that it is both politic and just—having regard to the progress of the useful arts—to provide some mode in which inventors may derive personal profit from their contributions to that progress, the next point to be ascertained is the *best* mode.

That which is the most obvious, is the payment by the state of a stated price or premium, but there are many and obvious objections to this mode. It could not be practically carried out with even justice to the public and to inventors, and it would entail a cumbrous and arbitrary system peculiarly open to abuse. It would be necessary either that the law itself should ascertain and fix valuations for inventions generally—manifestly an absurd and impractical thing, and one which, if attempted, would work injustice, sometimes to the public, and sometimes to inventors,—or the fixing of values must be left to tribunals, whose decisions would, of necessity, be arbitrary and unsatisfactory, since they could not apply to the determination of the question the only reasonable and just test, that of experience.

These, and other objections equally obvious, but to which it is not to our purpose here to allude, make it plain that a system of this kind would not well answer the end of promoting the progress of the useful arts.

The objections which we have cited, going to show what is *not* a good and efficient mode, point to the principles necessarily governing a mode which *is so*

It is just and proper that a new and useful invention should be paid for *by* the public, in proportion to its proven value *to* the public, and that the mode of valuation should be the same as in the case of other products of individual skill and labor.

The public verdict, as evidenced in demand, is the best general test of the value of an article, and the profit derived from manufacture and sale, if these be carried on with proper enterprise and discretion, will be in proportion to the value.

This is the philosophy of that mode of paying inventors which is known as the patent system; a mode the most just and reasonable that could be devised.

Letters-patent grant to the inventor of a new and useful improvement the exclusive right, for a stated period, of making, using, and selling such improvement

If an invention thus secured for a time by patent be really valuable and important, it is of course desirable that it should be brought into public use as speedily and widely as possible, and here the interests of the public, and those of the inventor are alike, for the advantage which the latter can derive from his patent, must altogether depend upon his diligence and discretion in availing himself of the exclusive right which it gives him. If, on the other hand, the invention be of no value and importance, the exclusive right of the inventor is altogether harmless; it will be practically no restraint upon the public, and will bring the inventor no more than he is entitled to.

Patents—in so far as they operate as a restraint upon the public—are yet decidedly beneficial restraints, for during the term of the inventor's exclusive right, the public are benefited in the *open* practice by the inventor himself, or those acquiring the right from him, of an invention, which, but for the prospect of that right, might not have been made, or having been made, might not have been disclosed. So far as the exclusive right operates as a tax upon the public, it is a tax justly proportionate to the ascertained value of the consideration given by the inventor; and after the exclusive right has expired, the public *freely* use the invention themselves, being enabled to do so by the knowledge which the inventor has imparted to them. These then are the principle and the object of a patent system: to promote the progress of the useful arts by extending to inventors that encouragement to exert their ingenuity, and disclose their inventions, which can be given with most advantage, both to the inventor and the community, in the shape of a temporary exclusive right to the former to make, use, and vend his invention.

Thus viewed, the patent laws assume the aspect of a compact between inventors and the public, by which the public in consideration of the disclosure by the inventor of an original thought which it is not compulsory upon him to disclose, yet of which, without such disclosure, neither he nor they can have the use and enjoyment, undertake to secure to him for a limited period, by positive grant, that exclusive right in his invention, which without such positive grant, it would be impossible for him to maintain.

The policy of patents as a means of promoting the progress of the useful arts, has been disputed, never seriously, however, in this country. In England the proposition has been made, and urged more loudly than forcibly, to abolish patents; but there the would-be abolitionists are a very small minority, and their views have been vigorously and successfully combated by some of the leading intellects of the country.

Holland stands alone as the country which has abolished patents. The abolition occurred in 1869, the royal proclamation stating that "the grants of exclusive rights for inventions and improvements or importations of objects of art and industry promote neither industry nor public interest."

In its experience on this subject, Holland seems to be as exceptional a country as it is in everything else. "Such a land as Holland," says a recent American writer, "exists nowhere else. It is not merely the most singular of kingdoms, it is the only one of its kind. You may travel the world over and yet be unable to form any conception of the Netherlands. You may live there your life long, and form no adequate idea of the remainder of the globe."

It is not at all unlikely that among a people so conservative and self-satisfied as the Hollanders, patent laws did not promote industry. The people, though robust, brave, and industrious, appear to have a horror of innovation, as is attested by their obstinate adherence to sleighs in place of wheeled vehicles, for drawing heavy loads over rough pavements. Little progress in the useful arts is to be expected in a country where men and horses continue to be shod with wood, and where men, women, and children are still to be found yoked to the same tow ropes with dogs and donkeys on the banks of the interminable canals.

It may be very true that the Dutch patent law did not promote the progress of the useful arts in Holland; great progress would scarcely be expected among a people so obstinately conservative, no matter what incentives were offered; but the Dutch law was so intensely selfish in its character that it would scarcely be expected to promote any public advancement in the arts, one of its prominent clauses being to the effect that a native forfeited his patent if he secured his invention in any other country.*

The patent abolitionists were unfortunate in pointing to the example of Holland, a country where the limited manufacturing interests are at a standstill, if not retrograding, and where the prominent products are gin, tulips, and cheese.

Switzerland, a country which never possessed any patent laws, is also pointed to by the advocates for the abolishment of patents. In respect to Switzerland, Mr. Day, in his able papers read before the Philosophical Society of Glasgow, papers from which we shall have to quote hereafter, says: "When do we hear of an important invention coming to maturity in this country? There is plenty of inventive talent in Switzerland, but Swiss inventors lack the stimulus of a patent law, and, therefore, have to come here or go elsewhere where an invention can be patented, and is recognized by the state as *bonâ fide* property."

To again quote from Mr. Day's book: "The patent system is the only one by which a nation can secure the maximum advantage from the invention, the only one by which invention is properly encouraged, the only one by which the real value of

---

* A Dutch legislator, in advocating the abolition of patents, declared that it was useless to point to the United States and England in support of Patent laws, because those countries were in a degenerate condition, not better than that of Holland at the close of the sixteenth century.

an invention can be ascertained, and, therefore, the only one which can secure not merely reward, but a due reward, precisely its exact worth to the inventor."

CHAPTER IV.

ESSENTIAL FEATURES OF A GOOD PATENT SYSTEM.

ASSUMING it to be politic and just to provide some mode in which the public shall pay inventors for their contributions to the progress of the useful arts, and that the best mode is by a properly devised patent system, we come next to consider what should be the characteristics of such a system. Undoubtedly the soundest patent law is that which treats inventors with the most liberality, on the plain grounds that the more liberal the law, the more it is likely to answer its public purpose of promoting the progress of the useful arts, by inducing the production and disclosure of new inventions.

But this idea of liberality to inventors is not to be carried so far, as to lose sight of the public object of the law, and of the fact, that having a reference to that object, inventors are simply the instruments and means. In other words, it is not to be forgotten that the utility of inventors to society is the consideration upon which the legal rights peculiar to them as inventors are based; that they occupy precisely the same footing as other producers to the public stock, and that society, in contracting to pay them, has the right to establish such provisions and conditions, as are necessary to assure that in each case the effect of the contract shall accord with its object and with the general welfare.

If these principles were continually and clearly borne in mind, we should have less of that criticism of the patent laws, based upon the false assumption, often expressed, that their one object is to "protect inventors." That is their end so far as concerns the *particular* interests of inventors, but they have a superior and public object, that of promoting the progress of the useful arts; with reference to this object, the "protection of inventors" is simply the means.

The proper liberality of the law to inventors is based not upon poetic sentimentality but upon perfectly utilitarian grounds and principles of practical justice.

Of the patent laws, therefore, as of any other contract, the justice is to be measured by the degree to which they appear to consult and reconcile the interests of all parties concerned, and to proceed upon the truth that the intended beneficial operation of the bargain must be destroyed by any provisions tending to antagonize the interests of the respective parties.

If this test be applied to our own patent system, we believe it will be found that the provisions and conditions which seem to be in the interests of the public, are also really to the advantage of inventors ; that the same precautionary measures work to the profit of both parties to the contract.

But before proceeding to apply the test, let us see what are the leading principles which, having due reference to the object to be attained, may be considered as essential to be recognized and followed by any sound patent law.

It is evident, to begin with, that *new and useful* inventions only, can be the subject of *valid* patents ; for if an inventor produce and disclose something which is not new, or something which cannot be used, or which it is against the interest of society to allow to be used, he simply gives society that which it had before, or that from which it can derive no benefit : which is to give nothing ; so that society owes him nothing. A patent, therefore, granted for such an invention, would be invalid for want of consideration.

Presuming the invention to be *new* and *useful*, it is no less essential to the validity of the patent that it shall have been fully and fairly disclosed by the inventor ; otherwise his part of the compact has not been carried out in good faith. There must be no concealment, no deception, but the information given must be sufficient to guide those skilled in the art to a beneficial use of the invention, so that the public may fully and freely advantage by it after the expiration of the patent.

In addition to this it is essential that the inventor shall have clearly pointed out and particularized what he claims to be original with him, that the public, during the existence of the patent, may be fully advised as to the nature and extent of the exclusive right which it confers, and as to what it is they are restrained from making, using, or selling, save with the permission of the patentee. As to this there should be no dissimulation, duplicity, or dubiousness, but a clear and candid statement of claim.

Now it is manifestly just both to the public and inventors to insure as far as possible that none but *valid* patents shall be granted ; that is to say, such as do in truth bestow that exclusive right which they *purport* to bestow.

This is just to inventors, because the value of patent property, as of any other, is in proportion to its ascertained degree of *certainty* and *security;* and just to the public, because the issue of *valid* patents only is plainly an important element in the efficiency and public advantage of a patent system.

It would seem then to be the important end to which the provisions of a patent law should *primarily* be directed, to confine the *issue* of patents as far as possible to inventions new and useful, clearly disclosed, and distinctly claimed.

A second object to be realized to

the fullest extent possible, consistently with the maintenance of the first, is that patents shall be easily, speedily, and cheaply attainable, so as to be within reach of rich and poor alike.

Here, too, the interests of the public and inventors are identical, for the more easily and cheaply *valid* patents can be obtained, the greater will be the number of new and useful inventions made and disclosed, and the more rapid in consequence the progress of the useful arts.

Naturally enough, inventors anxious to obtain their patents, and inclined to look upon the grant as matter of natural right, are apt to look upon this second object as the most important. But a little reflection will convince them that the matter of prime importance to them is the degree of confidence which they can place in the *validity* of their patents, and that a reasonable expense of time and money in necessary proceedings to ascertain, before a patent is granted, that it shall have the essentials to validity, is beneficial to themselves.

In this regard, too, the interests of inventors and the interests of the public are the same.

It is to the advantage of both— it is the right of both—that, while the issue of *valid* patents shall be as free as possible, the execution of the law shall yet be so regulated that the smallest possible number of *invalid* patents shall escape into existence.

CHAPTER V.

THE AMERICAN PATENT SYSTEM. PREVIOUS OFFICIAL EXAMINATION.

WE now come to the consideration of the more immediate subject of this treatise,—the merits of the American patent system. And first, as to that examination into the *novelty* and *utility* of an invention before granting a patent, which is the main distinguishing feature of the system. This peculiarity is a recognition of the principle to which we have above referred, that the *first* point of importance, both to the public and to inventors, is to provide for ascertaining, *before* a patent is granted, that the invention is new, useful, and clearly described and claimed.

But perhaps the intent and effect of this previous examination can best be understood by comparison with foreign systems, of which it forms no part; that of England, for example.

In England patents are, to all practical intents and purposes, granted for the asking, without inquiry as to whether the inventions sought to be patented are either new or useful, or sufficiently described.

The time and mode for determining these questions are after the grant of the patent, through the medium of court or jury.

It is plain, therefore, that an English patent carries with it no presumption of validity, unless, having undergone thorough scrutiny in the course of litigation, it has been indorsed by court or jury.

Of what satisfaction and value to the inventor, it may be asked, is a patent upon which he cannot place, nor expect others to place, any degree of confidence, unless it shall have successfully passed through the fire of litigation.

Such a system is a departure from the true principles of good legislation, whose highest office it is to cut off sources of litigation.

For this end are designed the numerous regulations which the laws provide, touching the acquisition, holding, and transmission of all kinds of property, with a view to ascertain, define, and publish the nature and extent of individual rights, that there may be the least possible occasion for those mistakes, and that confusion or conflict of claims from which litigation springs.

And certainly patent property should not be excepted from, but should rather receive an unusual degree of this solicitude of the law, for it is property which the law itself has created for the public benefit, and which, therefore, not only public policy but public good faith requires should be most carefully and tenderly guarded from the mischiefs of litigation.

The English patent law, therefore, in making litigation *necessary* to raise any practical presumption of the validity of a patent, is certainly an anomalous law.

An English patent which has not yet been successfully litigated is naturally an object of doubt and suspicion—a state of affairs productive of two classes of evils: First, the very inferior value of patents as negotiable property, an evil which that large class of inventors lacking capital will readily appreciate; and, second, the constant and aggravated violation of patent rights which must ensue from the general disregard in which those rights, from their uncertainty, are held.

It is manifest that under such a system the field of patent property is a mere scrambling-ground, with all the odds in favor of the wealthy and the unscrupulous. A poor patentee will be fortunate indeed if he is able to make his patent a source of profit to himself; the chances are that he will be driven to his election whether quietly to submit to the wholesale piracy of his rights, or whether dearly to purchase the alliance of capital for the maintenance of those rights at the sacrifice of the lion's share in them.

In this way patents, while they may serve to enrich the rich, are a very doubtful blessing to the poor. The privilege which such a patent confers, is, substantially, the privilege of establishing a right, if one can, by a lawsuit, a species of investment in litigation in which none but a litigious man can find enjoyment, and none but a wealthy man can indulge.

It is true, that the inventor of a

really valuable improvement may find some protection in the enterprise of capitalists desirous of obtaining the benefit of it, but this is an accidental and not always desirable sort of protection.

It is, perhaps, one of the strongest possible arguments in favor of a patent system, that the English system, inefficient and unjust, as in many respects it is, and very expensive, has yet undoubtedly done much to foster the practical arts, and is resorted to by a large number of inventors.

Such evils as we have indicated, the system of previous examination adopted by our law is intended to obviate as far as possible. Absolutely to remove patent or any other property from the region of doubt and litigation is impossible, and however perfectly adapted to this end the theory of a law may be, its administration must, if only from unavoidable errors of judgment, fall short of attaining a practical realization of that theory. We say this because of the complaints and criticisms which have from time to time been directed against our law; undoubtedly the majority have arisen from particular instances of failure or shortcoming in the *administration* of the law.

It is not our purpose here to contend that the past or present administration of the examining system was or is perfect, or so nearly perfect as it might be. It is no doubt the case that the capacity of the machinery of administration has not kept pace with the rapidly growing demand upon it, and time and experience have suggested, and will continue to suggest desirable additions and modifications in detail.

But from the complaints, just and unjust, made against the administration of the examining system, have been deduced arguments that the system itself is a failure, a positive disadvantage and should be abolished.

The very doubtful soundness of a conclusion thus arrived at is pretty apparent. It is not a fair conclusion, unless it be shown that the defects of administration are not the accidents liable to arise in any administration, but are defects originating and inherent in, and inseparable from the very nature of the particular system administered. When it is shown that the best attainable means of administration have been tried and have resulted in the same faults and defects as inferior means, then it is allowable to assume that the system cannot be administered, and should be abolished; but in this case the complaints, so far as they are true, are such as indicate very possible improvements of administration.

Since, however, this subject of the advantage or disadvantage of an examining system is one of great importance and has attracted much discussion *pro* and *con*, it is worth while to look into the complaints which have been urged against our system to see how far these complaints are justifiable, and entitled to the great weight which has been given to them.

It is necessary, first, to strip the question of a very common fallacy, arising from an utter misunderstanding of the law, but which is often advanced as a proof that the system of previous examination is not effective. It is undoubtedly the fact that an exceedingly large proportion of patents granted are for trifling things, or for things valueless, because inferior to previously existing things, for the same or a similar purpose. Now, it is asked, why does the government, which pretends to grant patents for new and *useful* inventions only, constantly issue patents in large numbers for useless and trifling notions? Such a question is simply an entire misapprehension of the intent of the law, and of the meaning of the word *useful* as employed in the statute. The word "useful" is not there synonymous with the word "valuable," nor does it indicate that an invention to be patentable must appear to be more efficient than, or even equally efficient with, prior inventions of the same class; but it simply means that to be patentable, an invention must be capable of use for some beneficial purpose, and not inoperative, vicious, or immoral. These are questions which can be decided soundly and justly by a competent tribunal, from the evidence afforded by the application for a patent.

But the *value* of an invention, which consists in its utility to the public at large, or more immediately to those concerned in that branch of art to which it relates, can evidently be determined only by time and experience in actual use; the only just verdict must be one rendered by the public from use; no law, nor man, nor set of men, can justly undertake to predetermine the question, since such a decision must necessarily be utterly arbitrary, and mere matter of opinion based upon insufficient evidence.

This point we have already undertaken to illustrate, in discussing the question of the proper mode of paying inventors for their contributions to the progress of the useful arts; and we observed that patents were the fairest mode, because in leaving the question of the *value* of each particular contribution open, to be decided in the only proper way, they give to the inventor the opportunity, by the exercise of ordinary diligence and discretion, of deriving a remuneration proportionate to that value, as thus most soundly tested and determined.

To be sure there are many cases in which ordinary perception and common sense, could without applying the tests of use and experience, soundly and justly determine the worthlessness of an invention, but in *all* cases such a mode of decision would be objectionable as arbitrary, and in *very many* cases would be at fault and unjust.

It would not be just to inventors generally, and there must be one rule of justice for all, to attempt to make this question of value a subject for legal or official decision, nor would it be in any way beneficial to the public. It is equally to their interest and to that of inventors, that every new idea should be allowed the test of practical experience. There is no reason why inventors should not have the same opportunity, as other producers, of submitting their productions to public arbitrament. Nor can patents for valueless inventions be objected to as working any legal injury to the public, for patents cannot practically operate as a restraint or as a tax upon the public with reference to things which, being of no advantage, they do not care to use.

There is no doubt that patents for valueless inventions have a mischievous effect in leading to lamentable wastes of valuable time and money; but this palpably is something for which the patent laws and their administration are in no way answerable. The evil in great measure arises from the very misapprehension of the law which we have been discussing, and which causes people to accept patents in the way of official evidence, which they are not, of the value of the things patented, and thus to conclude that they are valuable, without inquiry or even against the evidence of their own senses. This of course is a voluntary error, for which the person in error is alone responsible.

And for the evil, so far as it arises from mere lack of discretion, or knowledge in individuals investing their time and money in patented inventions, to hold the patent system responsible, or to draw therefrom an argument against that system, is about as reasonable and logical as though a man, having stupidly wasted his money upon a poor piece of land, should cast the blame upon Nature for having placed the land *in his way.*

It is true that our Patent Act authorizes the Commissioner to issue patents where he shall find the inventions sufficiently useful and important, and this might seem to give the Commissioner a discretion capable of much latitude in its exercise, in adjudging as to the patentability of inventions. But this discretion is to be exercised in accordance with the known policy and principles of the law—as judicially settled—and the inquiry of the Commissioner is to proceed no further than to ascertain that the invention has that negative sort of utility which is necessary for the *support* of a patent if granted.

"By useful invention in the statute (said Judge Story) is meant such a one as *may be* applied to some use; beneficial to society in contradistinction to an invention which is injurious to the morals, the health, or the good order of society. It is not necessary to establish that the invention is of such general utility as to supersede all other inventions now in practice, to accomplish the same purpose. It is sufficient that it has no noxious or mischievous tendency, that it may be applied to practical uses, and that so far as it is applied it is salutary. *If its practical utility be very limited, it will follow that it will be of little or no profit to the inventor; and if it be trifling, it will sink into utter neglect.* The law, however, does not look to the DEGREE of utility; it simply requires that it shall be capable of use, and that the use is such as sound morals and policy do not discountenance or prohibit."

The same doctrine is enunciated in numerous decisions, and points clearly to the bounds of the Commissioner's discretion in this matter. It extends no further than that, before issuing a patent, he should satisfy himself that the invention has utility as distinguished from utter impracticability or noxious tendency, and importance as distinguished from absolute frivolity. The question of *value* then, in its ordinary relative signification, the patent laws very properly do not bring into consideration as in any way entering into the question of an inventor's legal title to a patent, and it is a fallacy to suppose that the system of previous examination is intended to inquire into or determine the point of *value* as thus understood.

Curiously enough upon this same fallacy is based a very common accusation of *injustice* against the examining system and its administration. It is often gravely objected, and was so but a short time since by one of our leading public journals, that the power conferred upon the officers of the patent office, of judging upon the *value* of inventions, is too arbitrary and dangerous a power.

So it would be if it did but exist. This objection in fact evidences a popular recognition of the truth which we have been endeavoring to illustrate, that an examining system extending to the question of *value* could not be justly administered. To the assertion that no such power exists, it may be replied that officers of the patent office have been known to exercise such a power. True enough, and this merely goes to show that among the numerous officials of the patent office some may, from time to time, be found who, from misunderstanding of duty, exceed their powers, and usurp an unlawful jurisdiction.

That ordinarily no such power is attempted to be exercised is best proven by the large number of patents issued for things of indifferent value or of no value at all. This fact, used as an argument against the efficiency of the examining system upon the hypothesis that an inquiry into value is part of that system, exposes at once the fallacy of that hypothesis, and that of the allegation of injustice based upon it.

Returning to the fact that officers of the Patent Office have been known to exceed their duty, by pronouncing judgment upon the value of inventions, this of course is a just ground of complaint, certainly, however, not against the examining system, in a departure from whose principles the wrong consists.

If the wrong were prevalent, there would be very good ground for asserting that the administration of the law was not in accordance with the law; but that the wrong is not prevalent the patent lists are convincing proof.

Still another very common fallacy is that which holds the examining system responsible for the many patents of little or no value, not because they refer to inventions of little or no value, but because the specifications and claims have been defectively and insufficiently drawn. This is something for which the patentees are alone responsible; it is at once their privilege and their duty to specify what it is they claim to have invented. The functions of the officers of the Patent Office are advisory no further than to ascertain before granting a patent that the alleged invention is intelligibly described, and that the claim made is certain and distinct. This much they must of necessity do in undertaking to look into the question of novelty and utility. And if the description be not sufficiently clear, or more is claimed than the applicant is entitled to, it is their duty to tell him so, that he may amend or modify his description or claim accordingly. But it is no part of their duty to volunteer information that less has been stated or claimed than might have been; this would be uniting the functions of judge and counsel, and assuming a duty which the law very properly leaves to the inventor himself. It is a fair presumption that the inventor is a competent guardian of his own interests, so far as concerns the disclosure of his own ideas, and the presentation of his own claim. That he will claim less than he *thinks* himself entitled to is not to be supposed. Nor does the case differ, though the inventor himself be incompetent to state his invention and claim with proper skill, for in such case it is incumbent upon him to seek the counsel of those who can perform this duty for him. The strict impartiality requisite to the faithful performance of the duties of an officer of the Patent Office must prohibit any such officer from placing himself in the position of an advocate for the inventor whose claim he is to pass upon. It is a common expression that the Patent Office is the guardian of the interests both of inventors and the public; and this is true so far as its meaning refers to the exercise of careful and impartial discrimination and judgment in passing upon claims of invention.

It is the duty of the Office to give the patent asked for, if the claimant appears entitled to it, or to give him information as to any facts which may appear to render the claim made inadmissible. The rest may well be left to the inventor himself, for he is to be dealt with as an *intelligent* man, capable of taking care of his own interests, and not as an incompetent under wardship.

CHAPTER VI.

ORDINARY CRITICISMS OF THE PATENT OFFICE CONSIDERED.

THE observations in the preceding chapter show that the true criterion by which the efficiency and justice of the examining system is to be measured, is not the number of patents for things of indifferent or no value, nor the number of patents with indifferent claims.

The true question is, how far has the administration of the examining system been successful in preventing the issue of patents for old or unpatentable inventions, or for inventions previously patented? and how far has its success in this direction been neutralized by accidents and shortcomings injurious to inventors and the public?

The efficiency of the administration of the Patent Office, in this regard, may be superficially illustrated by official figures. Thus taking the Commissioner's report for 1870, we find in that year 19,171 applications for letters-patent were made, and it would appear that an average of a little over one-fourth as many were rejected for want of patentability, chiefly of course for lack of *novelty*. Supposing all these rejections to have been for just and sufficient cause, the system in the year 1870 saved the public and inventors from the issue of nearly 5000 invalid patents.

But it is not pretended that these figures show the actual state of the case. We cite them here as a species of starting-point and guide in estimating the weight of the various pertinent criticisms urged against the examining system and its administration. These criticisms may be divided into three classes.

1st. That patents are granted for old things, or for things previously patented to others, or for *unpatentable* things.

2d. That patents are refused for things which are patentable.

3d. That unnecessary expenses and delays are occasioned in the procuring of patents.

Without denying that there is truth in each and every one of these complaints, we propose to show that from the very nature of things the evils complained of have been greatly exaggerated; that so far as they have existed beyond that degree which it would perhaps be impossible to avoid, they are traceable to certain defects of organization which may be cured; and that they have been altogether overbalanced by the good which the system, though imperfectly administered, has nevertheless worked.

Coming first to the charge that despite the examining system, patents are granted for old things, or things previously patented to others, or unpatentable.

In the first place it is well to remember, both in reference to this and to other grounds of complaint, that they originate in particular instances, and while such instances are much bruited, from the injury real or fancied to individuals, the evidences of efficiency in the administration of the examining system, rest in official records which meet the eyes of comparatively few.

The official figures which we have cited are really evidences of general efficiency of vastly more weight than any adverse evidence to be derived from the isolated experiences of individuals, yet the latter are more openly noised, and from this reason alone receive a degree of credit which a moment's consideration of the other side of the question would serve to take from them.

Nor should it be forgotten how far charges of this nature may rest on mere *opinion*, and that, interested opinion. Take the case of a prior patentee and a present applicant for a patent, whose several inventions border very closely upon each other, all the probabilities are that if the opinions of the respective parties were taken they would prove diametrically opposite; the patentee would insist on the identity or equivalency of the two devices, the applicant would see a clear difference between the two, and instance the refusal of a patent to him as a piece of rank injustice and stupidity on the part of the Office. Each party would see and argue in his own interest.

Nor is interest the only cause of error in this matter; it is by no means an uncommon incident for impartial men, equally expert, to differ in their views as to the substantial identity and equivalency of devices, or as to their patentability.

This shows that in considering this class of complaints, much allowance is to be made for difference of judgment, and with the caution that the most interested judgment is not the most likely to be correct.

Then again, it is a necessary feature of the patent law, not so generally understood as it should be, that changes or additions, be they ever so trifling apparently, in existing devices, whether patented or not, are entitled to letters-patent if they involve any degree of invention, to be determined mainly by the test of result.

Many a patentee discovering that some one has patented an improvement upon his invention, an improvement which no doubt to him seems more questionable or trifling than it may to others, is filled with resentment, first at the presumed poacher upon his fancied domain, and next at the Patent Office for allowing and indorsing the imagined intrusion. This is all wrong, but is loudly insisted on, in proportion to its wrongfulness. It arises mainly from the one grand fallacy, that the patent laws are intended, not for the benefit of the public at large, but for that of inventors in particular. Nor does a patentee thus complaining usually stop to reflect, that, but for the examining system he so bitterly accuses, the subsequent patent, in which the fancied injury lies, might have embraced not only the improvement, but also his own invention, thus working a substantial mischief, to be abated perhaps only by litigation.

It is complained that many rejections are not for just and sufficient cause, and that inventors are often refused patents for that which is patentable. As to this particular complaint it is to be observed that failures to obtain a patent for that which is patentable, cannot be fairly charged as failure of justice until it be shown that every means which the examining system provides for obtaining his claim has been exhausted by the inventor in vain. This removes from the category of cases in point, those in which the inventor has not elected to exercise his right of appeal from a first or second adverse judgment. Thus the number of pertinent examples is very materially reduced.

It may be safely asserted that a critical and impartial judgment would find those cases very few indeed in which a *just* claim of invention, properly presented and prosecuted as far as possible, has been refused.

But it is further complained that improper rejections by subordinate officers drive applicants to the expense and delay of appeals, or lead to the abandonment of applications, or where they do not have one of these effects, still cause unnecessary expenditure of time and trouble in obtaining patents. There is truth in this complaint, and we shall have occasion to discuss the causes of the evil. But our present purpose is to point out to those who would enter upon a consideration of the examining system and its administration impartially, certain facts and reasons tending greatly to diminish the real weight of these complaints.

It is first to be noted that appeals, whether justly or unjustly occasioned, are exceptional. It is a fact that the great majority of patents issued are allowed by the officers to whom the cases are first referred. In these instances, presuming the inventor to have performed his part of the duty by presenting his claim in proper and intelligible form, the process, expense, and time required are in general as simple, moderate, and brief as possible. It is a question which we shall have occasion to inquire into, whether the extreme simplicity and facility do not work injustice of another kind to the public and inventors; but the alleged injustice with which we are now dealing is that of expense and delay.

As to abandonment of applications, it is to be said, that in most cases it is *voluntary*, arising either from the applicant's ignorance of his rights, or from indifference or want of energy, in either of which cases the fault is his own. It may be admitted that the mistakes of examiners have on rare occasions led to the involuntary abandonment of just claims. Such cases must be exceedingly few, since the fees for appeals are so small as to be within the command of almost every one.

As to difficulties being cast in the way of obtaining patents by the *mistakes* of officers, there is vastly more substance in this branch of the complaint than in the other. At the same time it is an evil which has been greatly exaggerated by the natural prejudices of inventors.

An inventor looking at patents in the fallacious light which we have been endeavoring to expose and controvert, and regarding himself as the only party interested in the patent laws, satisfied, too, in his own mind, with or without inquiry, that his invention is new and useful, and that a patent is his right, chafes at what he considers, in *his* particular case at least, to be a useless delay. The same man, having real estate to sell, would hardly expect any one to purchase without taking the time to satisfy himself upon the question of title. Let him reflect then that the public, in granting him a patent for his invention, does so by way of purchase, and that, unless his invention be new and useful, he has nothing to sell, the public, in providing that its officers shall take necessary time and proceedings to determine these questions before consummating the bargain, is doing simply what any business man would do in like case.

It is an important fact to be remembered too, that of the delays and expenses incurred through rejections of applications, a very large percentage is due to the informal, imperfect, and unskilful preparation and presentation of such applications by inventors or their representatives. This is a fruitful cause of difficulty of which little is heard for very obvious reasons; it is a cause likely to be overlooked, or at least not openly acknowledged by the parties to whom it is due.

It is the prevalent error in these complaints of expense and delay, that they are directed against the Patent Office indiscriminately, without perception of, or reference to, their true causes. Occurring *in* the Office, they are charged *to* the Office; and to this not only the natural impatience of inventors leads, but the conceit or the lack of candor of many of a large body of professional men.

This is not to be wondered at while there is among so large a proportion of inventors, a one-sided and partial understanding of the nature and object of the patent laws.

This leads them to measure the justice and efficiency of the administration of the laws solely by the ease and readiness with which patents are allowed, a test so obviously wrong, that nothing more need be said about it.

That this should be the case with inventors is not perhaps to be wondered at, but it is a somewhat astonishing and discreditable fact, that this false sentiment is echoed and encouraged by some of those whose profession it is to make and prosecute the applications of inventors.

That an inventor should find in every unexpected lapse of time or dollar of expense incurred in the attainment of his wishes an instance of personal injury and a cause of complaint is not unnatural, but for a man, whose profession should bespeak a fair understanding of the law, and a cool judgment, to adopt or to counterfeit the like hot-headed, misjudging impatience, speaks little for his capacity or his candor.

While thus contending that the class of complaints with which we have been dealing, have received a degree of weight and credit, to which they are by no means entitled, we would not be understood as denying that there have been some just grounds for such complaints. Such legitimate causes, though on examination they will be found to be infinitely fewer than may be commonly supposed, are yet more numerous than need be, and while they do not serve to point the extravagant arguments which have been based upon them, they do serve to indicate very possible improvements of administration.

CHAPTER VII.

ACTUAL DEFECTS OF THE PRESENT ORGANIZATION OF THE PATENT OFFICE AND THE REMEDY.

HAVING seen how strongly the ordinary criticism of the administration of the examining system is from the very nature of things tinctured by interest and mistaken prejudice, and how much of it is based upon opinion, not always the most competent or impartial, let us next see what evils the most impartial inquiry will be disposed to allow, either as existing or as threatening, and inquire whether they are of such a nature, and so mischievous that their existence or probability presents a fair argument against the wisdom of the system.

The object of the system, as we have seen, is to ascertain at a time most advantageous to the public and to the inventor, that is, before a patent is granted, whether the subject sought to be patented is *legally* patentable.

The questions to be looked into may be stated generally as the novelty and utility of the invention, but these embrace a variety of questions, requiring for their proper solution, experienced and sound judgment.

The most obvious labor which the system involves is that of research; for the thorough and impartial performance of this duty, it will not be denied, an organization like that of the Patent Office is most admirably adapted.

It is in the assumption of this duty by the public through its designated officers, that the real benevolence of the examining system is most strikingly apparent; for inventors individually to make the researches necessary to determine with any degree of satisfaction whether their inventions are new or old, would in most cases be utterly impracticable, and could not be attempted save at enormous cost of time and money. In applying the moderate fees asked of applicants for patents to the collection and compact and systematic arrangement of the means for readily making these researches, and to the payment of a sufficient number of officers to make them, when it is most to the advantage of inventors that they should be made, the law proceeds upon principles of true liberality and justice.

But the proper application of these researches involves judgment upon matters of diverse natures, requiring for their consideration different kinds of knowledge and experience.

The question of novelty is not one merely of the apparent similarity or diversity of things in matter of form or constituent parts or operation, it is not a question addressed merely to the eye or ear.

The questions of novelty and utility are naturally blended thus far, that inventions are really *new* inventions, entitling their inventors to be treated as producers to the public stock, only when useful in the sense of availability to some beneficial end.

It therefore often becomes a matter for nice discrimination and judgment to determine whether the points of apparent difference between one device and another involve this utility, and so go to constitute patentable novelty, or whether they are mere barren changes of no effect.

And apart from its bearing upon the question of novelty, that of utility is in itself, one for the intelligent consideration of which a high degree of knowledge and discretion is often required.

Then as the law has specified different classes of patentable subject-matter, it frequently becomes necessary to decide under which of them, a particular invention is properly to be classed, and whether therefore it is or is not patentable as described and claimed by the applicant.

And as the first inventor only of a new and useful device is entitled to a patent, the questions to be de cided in the Patent Office are not only those which in every case exist between claimants and the public, but those also which frequently arise between different claimants of the same invention. These are judicial questions requiring for their proper determination a knowledge of general and of patent law.

The various questions then, which necessarily arise in the administration of an examining system, require the union within the Office of different capacities and accomplishments; there must be diligent research, there must be capacity to judge upon questions of fact touching matter in the various practical arts, and there must be capacity correctly to apply the law to the various states of fact.

Applications for letters-patent are very numerous, they relate to many different branches of art, and in their consideration, as we have seen, many questions of diverse kinds arise.

For the administration therefore of the examining system, an extensive organization is required embracing many officials.

Now the evils likely to arise in such a state of affairs will readily suggest themselves; they are the dangers incident to any organization embracing various classes of duties, the proper performance of some of which requires that they should concentrate in the hands of a few, of others that they should be divided among many.

An improper division of labor without due regard to the capacities required for its proper performance; the intrusting of that to many which could be more satisfactorily performed by a few; the improper conjunction of opposite duties, some executory, others discretionary and judicial, some requiring chiefly time and diligence, others requiring special knowledge and capacity, and the too general dispersal of important powers.

Such mischiefs as these are likely, if not carefully provided against, to creep into any such organization, and to cause conflicts, confusion, and lack of uniformity, exposing the whole structure to the charge of cumbrousness and inefficiency.

Into such mischiefs and its consequent accusation has the Patent Office in fact, to some extent, justly fallen.

In looking for the cause of this we may proceed upon the principle, heretofore indicated, that the labor of the Patent Office is of two kinds, one calling for intelligent research, the other for judgment.

The chief requisites for the proper performance of the first class are time, diligence, and division of labor; for the second, the wants are learning and capacity, and so far as possible, concentration of authority. Division, so far from being a necessity here, is a grave objection, and for the evident reason, that in matters of judgment affecting important interests the desiderata are *certainty* and *uniformity*.

Any one aware of the present constitution of the Patent Office will admit that these principles have not in practice been recognized to that extent which the law originally contemplated.

In the early days of the Patent Office, when inventions were comparatively few, the labor and authority were placed in the hands of one or two men. The demand on the Office grew more rapidly than had been anticipated, and the necessity for a division of labor became apparent. It was a natural though a mischievous result, that with the division of labor there was also a division of authority, which necessarily resulted in a want of uniformity in the practice of the Office.

In 1855, Judge Mason, then Commissioner of Patents, perceived the difficulties which had even then, when there were but twelve principal examiners, arisen from this subdivision of independent judicial action. The judge said, in his report, "There are very grave objections to a further increase of the number of principal examiners. The system has already overgrown in that respect, and seems almost imperatively to demand some modification to give it a proper harmony and uniformity of action. They (the examiners) act to a considerable extent independently of each other, and possessing very different minds and views they follow different rules of action and decision."

To-day, we see the duties and the powers originally designed to be exercised by one man or at least by a few men, acting *in conjunction*, divided among more than a score of officers acting *independently* of each other, and what is worse, to a great degree independently of the really responsible power of the Office.

It is here that the evil lies, and the parties injured are not merely those from whom the loudest cries of injury are heard, not those impatient men who measure the justice and efficacy of the system by the ease and readiness with which the Office may coincide with their views and gratify their wishes, but the public, and those patentees whose interests—measured by the value of their contributions to the practical arts—are of great weight.

To the rights or presumed rights of applicants, the power of appeal gives ample protection against the adverse action of any of the score of examiners, but the rights of the public and those of prior patentees have no such protection.

Yet there can be no doubt that this defect in the organization of the Patent Office is really also of serious injury to applicants for patents. While it does not necessarily tend to ultimate and permanent injustice, it certainly does tend to vexatious trouble and delay, in themselves grave injustice.

Plainly the existence of a large number of *nominally* subordinate but *in effect* independent officers, each one of them uniting in himself executive and judicial functions, and this without that direct responsibility which should attach to such functions—officers whose actions are to a great extent uncontrolled by the authority with whom is placed the responsibility for the proper administration of the law—presents an anomalous and mischievous state of affairs. Every officer may constitute a little court of his own, and may adopt his own maxims of law and of practice, and it will be a marvel in the history of human nature if the disposition to do this is not in an inverse ratio to the real capacity and responsibility of the man.

This is an evil fruitful of doubt and delay, needlessly embarrassing inventors in the presentation and prosecution of their claims, provocative of prejudice and irregular practice, and it is an evil of which in the present organization of the Office, there is constantly increasing danger. Fortunately, as a rule, the officers of the Patent Office have, considering the temptation and the opportunity, been signally free from dangerous assumptions of authority.

Far from attributing the want of uniformity in the action of the Patent Office, and the evils resulting therefrom, to the officers of that Bureau personally, we should be doing an injustice to many accomplished gentlemen who have occupied, or who now occupy, the responsible position of Examiner, if we failed to record our opinion that the degree of uniformity of action is, considering the circumstances, somewhat astonishing, and may be charged to the good sense and ability of these officers as a rule, and to their observance of the instructions derived during the last few years from able heads of the Office.

True there have been, and will probably continue to be, examiners with perverted ideas; men who consider they are best performing their duties by presenting every obstruction to the grant of patents by technical objections and trifling actions; others again, who will manufacture patent law of their own, and others who through a spirit of display will apply theoretical dogmas derived from collegiate cramming in cases where practical knowledge and common sense would be a much more available means of arriving at a correct judgment. These officers are the exception, but the mischief they have caused, and continue to cause, is great, so great as to reflect more or less odium on the whole examining corps, so that the many intelligent officers have had to bear the brunt of objections attributable to the freaks of the few.

Undoubtedly this division of power has worked great mischief to applicants for patents, and for the same reasons that it has worked still greater mischiefs to the public and to patentees. It creates too many irresponsible judges, and unites too various functions in the same officers without due reference to the various capacity and knowledge required. The nature of the resulting mischief varies with the character of the officers, the tendency of whose errors will be in some cases to grant patents which should not be granted, in others to withhold them when they should be granted, and thus action will become regulated rather by personal character and whim, than by any fixed and clear principles.

This will all the more be the tendency because the powers which these officers separately exercise are of a nature requiring for their proper exercise a *union* of capacities and attainments not commonly found in one mind. The questions of fact, and of mixed fact and law, constantly coming up for consideration, call both for scientific and practical, and for legal knowledge and judgment. It is in the latter branch that the examiners are most likely to be deficient, as their selection is supposed to be governed by their presumed knowledge in the various branches of the practical arts.

Legal reasoning is not to be expected from those not grounded in legal principles; and there is no branch of the law admitting of more refined and subtle distinctions, requiring a more delicate and skilful handling than that relating to patents. "Patents," said Judge Story, "are the very metaphysics of the law." It is not one of the least alarming signs of the system as now conducted, that the application of the law to a subject so delicate and so important as that of invention, is so largely left to a number of men of whom many will have no better guide in their attempted application of judicial doctrine than the letter of Law Reports, whose spirit they cannot grasp.

The necessary union of qualifications is not likely to be found in each one of more than a score of men.

But even suppose that this end could be accomplished, still the present organization of the Office would be defective; for where there is not coaction there cannot be unanimity, and especially in regard to a subject where so much difference of opinion may arise among the most expert and intelligent minds.

But is the evil incapable of remedy or avoidance? The nature of the remedy is indicated by the nature of the evil; but there may be those who will doubt the feasibility of applying the remedy. A return to the original constitution of the Office is of course impossible, but surely a return to original principles is not. If the duty of research, requiring time and diligence, were more completely separated than now rom that of judgment, which requires rather knowledge and tact, the result would be a more satisfactory performance of both duties. United in the same hands, the two duties become a mutual embarrassment; they are diverse in nature, call for different kinds and degrees of mental capacities and attainments, and he who may most satisfactorily perform the one may be most unfitted for the other. For the labor of research, that which requires time and numbers, the present organization of the Office, with its very complete subdivisions, is perhaps as good as could be devised, and its efficiency would be greatly increased by the more complete separation of this class of labor from the other.

And as for what may be termed the judicial part of the duty, plainly it could be more speedily and satisfactorily performed by a few men acting in union, and having laid before them the evidence upon which they are to form their judgment, than it can possibly be by a much larger number of men acting independently and having with the duty of judging that also of looking up the evidence. The responsibility which attaches to judgment would in this way rest with a small body of men, selected for their capacity, acting in union, and not diverted from the efficient performance of their duties by labor which could as well be performed by another class of officers. Thus the practice of the Office would be more thorough, more efficient, and more uniform.

It is not our purpose to suggest the legislation which may be required, or the details of a mode, for working this desirable change. We have simply undertaken to point out wherein the real evils of the organization as it now is, exist and have their origin, and the principles which it would seem should govern any endeavor to remedy and obviate such evils.

The perfect feasibility of carrying out these principles will hardly be disputed, but what legislation and what changes would best carry them out, is a matter in which there may well be diversity of opinion.

We have only to add that the present accomplished head of the Office, from whom we have received valuable information, has every faith in the perfect feasibility and absolute necessity of carrying out these principles, and his opportunities of judging of the want of uniformity of action, together with his past able administration of the Office, point to him as the one most able to judge as to what legislation may be required to correct an evil which, if permitted to grow, must eventually undermine our Patent System.

CHAPTER VIII.

BENEFITS OF AN EXAMINING SYSTEM.

WHILE recognizing the defects in the present organization of the Patent Office, and the evils which have ensued from them, and which are likely to grow unless speedily checked, we are not of those who discover in the past history of the organization any such traces of inherent mischief as serve to indicate impracticability in an examining system.

On the contrary we contend that the past administration of the examining system has been productive of good, entirely outweighing the evil.

We have adduced certain official figures which show that in the year 1870 to a little more than 19,000 applications made, the number rejected was nearly 5000.

Now supposing that but one-third even of these rejections were on proper grounds, or need have been acquiesced in by the applicant, what saving of time, and money, and labor, that might otherwise have been thrown away in fruitless enterprise or litigation, do more than fifteen hundred rightfully rejected cases in the course of one year represent; what value in protection to the respectability and consequent value of patent property in general, is represented by the withholding in one year of fifteen hundred patents, which, granted, would not have been worth the paper on which they were printed.

These are points which are apt to escape consideration, yet when brought to mind they are very suggestive.

Then turn to another effect of the examining system, defectively administered as it may be; we allude to what may be termed its advisory and restraining effect. It is the very clear interest of inventors to claim all that they imagine themselves entitled to, and this is exceedingly likely to be more than in fact they *are* entitled to. Claims often include with that which is new, that also which is old, and either public property or the property of some prior patentee. No candid man, having experience in these matters, will deny that the administration of the examining system has worked almost incalculable good to applicants, to patentees, and to the public, in pointing out and checking these unwitting or deliberate intrusions upon public or appropriated ground, and indicating the real bounds of invention. This service has protected the interests of many a patentee, has thrown much needed light upon many an inventor's path, has tempered his too buoyant anticipations before they had led him into expenditures and enterprises, which blindly pursued, would have resulted in complications, loss, and bitter disappointment, and in every such saving to inventors is reflected a saving to the public.

And there is still another benefit necessarily proceeding from examination, a benefit of such importance that it might in itself be deemed an *offset* to many mischiefs. We refer to the necessity for clear and full specifications, and precise claims.

The scrutiny which, in examination, descriptions and claims undergo, must act as an effectual curb upon carelessness, duplicity, and vagueness in their preparation. An applicant must, in his own interest, be frank and precise in his statements, and thus a general correctness is engendered, the importance of which to public and private interests cannot be overestimated. There cannot be in American patents that indefiniteness or vague generality of description and claim which is so conspicuous in many foreign patents, and which at once requires litigation to unravel, and renders litigation tedious, expensive, and unsatisfactory.

And who can estimate the value of the Patent Office records, under the examining system, in respect to the light which they serve to throw on the legal status and the commercial value of patents? Upon every patent issued, the record of the application, of the rejections it may have met, the reasons for these rejections, the references given to prior inventions, forms a compact commentary, which, while at times it may only show how singularly at fault the official judgment has been, is yet calculated to be of invaluable service in aiding and guiding those who may desire to judge for themselves to what extent the value of a patent is affected by what has gone before.

Nor will it escape the notice of the impartial critic that the administration of the examining system, with all its imperfections and shortcomings, has done very much to give to patents, as was intended, a higher legal and commercial status than they have in any other country. That *is* certain, which can be made certain, and every aid to arriving at certainty is of moment. How much of that all-important element, certainty, must be given to patent property by the means of arriving at it which the Office records furnish!

There can be no doubt that the moral weight, the weight of presumption which letters-patent here carry with them into the courts, and among that portion of the public who have any understanding of the Patent System, has done very much, not only to simplify and economize, but to cut off litigation by inspiring confidence on the side of right, and caution upon that of wrong.

Nor has this moral power as we may term it, of patent property, decreased, as, if the administration of the examining system were on the whole a failure, it must have done, in proportion to the marvellous increase in the quantity of such property existing, although it has doubtless fluctuated with the apparent competence and honesty, or their opposites, in the ruling powers at the Patent Office.

The Patent Office is a very extensive institution, in which is collected a vast amount of material, rapidly augmented by constant accessions. This fact has led many to regard the organization as one which if not already cumbrous and unwieldy, must speedily become so, and alarming pictures have been given of the tremendous accretions of matter. It is asked how is it possible for men to conduct searches with speed and certainty amidst such records. Much has already been done to solve the question, by division of material and labor, by reducing the records to compact and accessible shape, and by elaborate classification, and no doubt experience will suggest further improvements in this direction. There is in truth no organization so large or complex, that a spirit of system and order cannot mould it into a simple and smoothly working unit. When the same correct principles have been applied to the arrangement of *duties* which have already worked such wonders in the arrangement of *material*, the Patent Office will become an example of efficiency and order and uniformity of action.

CHAPTER IX.

THE EXAMINING SYSTEM AS VIEWED FROM ABROAD.

While upon the subject of an examining system it will not be out of place to see how it is regarded abroad, since the foreign views of the subject have been largely governed by observance or report of the effect of the system as administered in this country.

We have already had occasion to refer to some of the peculiarities and defects of the English Patent System, which have recently attracted great attention. The subject has been much discussed both in and out of Parliament, and committees of inquiry have had before them the testimony of many prominent men, whose position, in respect to the practical arts, or whose legal attainment entitle their opinions to great consideration.

The defects of the present English system are generally acknowledged, and seem to have divided those taking part in the discussion into two parties: 1. Those who would abolish patents altogether, and 2. Those who, favoring patents, yet perceiving the deficiency of the present laws, proposed a variety of remedial measures.

Of the former parties the number is not large, nor the reasoning such as to carry *any* weight with it.

Apart from the great cost of patents, the one great deficiency of the law, admitted on all sides, lies in the practically indiscriminate and uncontrolled issue of patents, which leaves *bonâ fide* inventors at the mercy, to a great extent, of unscrupulous pirates, and opens the door to patents for merely pretended inventions, or for absurd and impracticable schemes, and of patents with insufficient, vague, and deceitful specifications and claims. Still worse,—there is no check upon the repeated patenting of similar inventions; and the rights of patentees are left in a cloud of darkness which litigation alone can break; this last evil being aggravated by insufficient means for trying patent causes.

The various remedies proposed agree in this,—that they all point to some mode of controlling the *issue* of patents, and the establishment of some special tribunal to deal with patent questions. As to the precise mode by which, and the time when, the ends aimed at should be attained, there seems to have been some difference of opinion.

Of course in a discussion of this kind our examining system did not escape attention, and its merits and defects, real or supposed, were freely canvassed.

It is worthy of note, however, that those who advocated the adoption in England of a system more or less analogous were men whose opinions were entitled to the greater weight, as they spoke from personal observation and experience.

Among these was Mr. Aston, a prominent barrister, who, after canvassing the defects of the English law, proceeds to suggest certain remedies; and speaking of them as being not merely speculative, but such as had been tried, thus remarks: "Those to which I attach the most importance have been fully tried in the United States of America, and found to work well. I mean *the exercise of discrimination in the grant of patents*, and what is still more important, the deposit before a patent is granted *of a precise description of the invention and claims*, given in a complete specification, which is submitted to a proper official examination before it is passed as sufficient. My own opinions upon the working of the American Patent Laws are founded upon a personal investigation of the system adopted in the United States, and from continued experience gathered in professional practice. My conviction is that the American system, though it has its imperfections, does work better than ours, *and that because it has cured in a great measure the defects under which our system is still laboring.*"

Mr. J. Howard, an inventor, manufacturer, and a Member of Parliament, while replying to the argument of those who would abolish patents altogether, remarked, that it appeared to him, that most of the arguments that had been urged did not touch the principles of a patent law, but *went rather to the defects of the existing law* and its administration. Mr. Howard took occasion to allude to the great and favorable impression which had been made on his mind by a visit to the United States Patent Office. He referred to the vital necessity for amendments in the English law, and expressed the hope that when the subject was taken in hand by the law officers of the Crown, *they would provide the means for a bonâ fide examination of all inventions before patents were granted;* and also provide that the specification should be so clear that the public may know what really the patent was granted for, and thus save the ruinous cost of legal proceedings.

Lord Romilly, Master of the Rolls, while among those inclined to the abolition of patents, on the theory that they had little to do with the progress of art and civilization, suggested as a remedy for the present inefficient state of the laws, "the appointment of a special tribunal of thoroughly efficient men, who should examine and pronounce upon all applications for patents, and grant them according as they might think the invention new and useful; or withhold them if the application was for what was trivial, worthless, injurious, or not new."

Still another advocate for the adoption in England of an examining system analogous to ours was found in the person of Mr. Mundella, himself a manufacturer of wide repute, and who has been a visitor in this country.

Of course argument against the adoption of such a system was not wanting. Reference was made to remarks proceeding, it would appear, some time ago, from Mr. Woodcroft, the accomplished Chief Clerk of the English Patent Office, whose invaluable services in superintending the publications of that office have gained him a well-earned repute. But Mr. Woodcroft's objections to an examining system seem to have been singularly unhappy in the supposed facts upon which they are based.

Said Mr. Woodcroft, "The Americans pay about £23,000 a year for preliminary examination, and they are very much dissatisfied with it. The system of preliminary examination has been tried and found wanting. It is in operation in Prussia, but does not give satisfaction. It was tried in France, Austria, Sardinia, and Belgium, but being most unsatisfactory, was abandoned in each country. It is now going on in America at an enormous expense, and the *Chief* Commissioner (?) wrote to me to say that it was a very inadequate system, and a very unfair one."

These remarks of Mr. Woodcroft's have been frequently quoted by opponents of the American examining system, and much greater importance has been attached abroad to the dictum of an ex-officer of our Patent Office, who is styled a *Chief Commissioner*, than we should be willing to accord to it here in view of the overwhelming opinions of our best authorities in favor of an examining system.

But we find Mr. Woodcroft, at a more recent date, saying: "Let every man have his patent, but before action is brought let the originality of the claim of the invention be sifted by the most competent men of the day," a theory to which we shall have occasion to refer to hereafter.

That in Prussia the system should have been a failure, no one will wonder when he reads the testimony of Mr. Bessemer, who speaks from experience of the honesty and benevolence of the working of the Prussian system, in regard to foreigners at least. Mr. Bessemer says that he did not take out a patent for his invention in Prussia, and explains the reason thus: "He sent his paper to Prussia in the care of Mr. Krupp, who paid him £5000 for the use of his patent. He applied in due course for a patent, and was informed by the Prussian Patent Office that the invention was not new. The Prussian Patent Office grant occasional patents; they take the fees and the drawings from British inventors in any case, and afterwards publish them for the benefit of Prussia. The Office said that Mr. Nasmyth was the inventor of the process; Mr. Nasmyth said he was not. They next said they would give the name of the real man in a few days. Six weeks passed, and they said, 'If we don't find the name of the real man to-morrow, we will give you a patent.' A week of these to-morrows passed, after which they showed an English blue-book *with his own invention published in it*, and they said, '*Your invention is published, so according to the law of Prussia we cannot grant you a patent.*' All the time they had been promising to grant it. The process is now worked very largely in Prussia."

It is to be hoped indeed that this was an extreme case in the working of the Prussian system, but it is a well-known fact that that system is utterly arbitrary both as to end and means, which is to say that it is necessarily and essentially a failure.

The example of Prussia, then, was a singularly unhappy and inapplicable argument against the adoption of a system of examination suited to a free country.

As to the failure of examining systems in France, Austria, Sardinia, and Belgium, in the absence of express information as to principles and details, the means adopted for carrying them out, or the extent of trial given them, it is not of course possible to examine into the causes of failure, but it would doubtless be found in the existence of some arbitrary features in either end or mode.

Returning to Mr. Woodcroft's theory, it will be seen that he is not opposed to an examining system, but to our system of examination in advance of the grant; he would grant any man a patent for anything, but before the patentee could exercise any rights against infringers of his patent, the latter must be submitted to the scrutiny of the "*most competent men of the day.*" If an examination is to be made, why should it not be in advance of the grant, so that the deed itself may be *prima facie* evidence of the patentee's rights? Why should one branch of the government indiscriminately grant patents for another branch to scrutinize before the patentees can go into court, or can go before the public with any ascertained rights? Why postpone locking the stable door till after the horse is out?

Curiously enough, ideas somewhat similar to Mr. Woodcroft's have prevailed, but to a very limited extent, in this country.

It has been proposed to continue an examining system, and if the Office refuses a patent to let the applicant take one on his own responsibility, the patent however to be accompanied with the taint of official refusal.

Of what earthly use would such a patent be to the holder, who would be in a position analogous to that of the man who bases his ownership to real estate on a deed either invalid on its face, or bearing such a taint that it is worthless?

Argument against the American system was also found in an article coming at secondhand from the columns of the "New York Tribune," quoted in other papers, both here and abroad.

This was the article to which we have had occasion to refer in an earlier part of this treatise as showing such an entire and singular misapprehension of the true principles of our system. The article animadverts upon the dangerous power exercised by our officials in pronouncing upon the novelty and VALUE of inventions;—"Power," says the article, "which the best functionaries might abuse through defect of information, or error in judgment, which the worst certainly will and do use most unrighteously."

That the law does not authorize inquiry into the *value* of inventions, we have shown, and as to the inquiry into novelty, is not the exercise of power in this respect sufficiently prevented, by the very nature of the inquiry, by the rights of the applicant to full information as to any cause of rejection, and by his right of appeal, from being improperly and unjustly exercised?

What must have been the surprise of those Englishmen who so keenly appreciated the evils of their patent system that they desired any mode of getting rid of it, even by the total abolition of patents, if no other way could be devised, to find this article gravely arguing that "our patent laws should be assimilated to the British; that the Patent Office should here, as there, simply register claims to have made inventions or discoveries in their order, and all questions thence arising should be taken to the courts and there settled."

Such a proposition as this must have given rise to the thought that the American examining system must be bad indeed, if it warrants the presenting to American inventors of this alternative as preferable.

The delightful results as they have been experienced in England, of treating property in invention as a bone to be carried off in triumph by the lucky winner among those who choose to fight for it, may be gathered from the testimony of Mr.

Nasmyth, the well-known inventor of the steam-hammer. "He had been called as a witness in patent cases, and had seen much of the advantages and disadvantages of patent litigation. He thought there was a natural tendency to partisanship among scientific witnesses, and had felt this tendency to become an advocate rather than a witness. His steam hammer had been infringed, but he took a commercial view of the matter. *He had seen so much of the enormous expense of litigation that he had always resolved to submit to any infringement rather than fight a battle at law.*"

Mr. Webster, a prominent barrister, characterized patent litigation as "nothing but speculations on the part of the litigants on the ignorance of the judge and jury; a jury is often very ignorant, and a judge more ignorant than all of them."

Other prominent and experienced men testified to like effect.

When we take into consideration the ambiguous character of many English patents, and the absence of definite claims, the ignorance of judges and juries is not much to be wondered at. In this country, however, a well-defined claim is demanded before the patent can issue; and in litigated cases the matters to be adjudicated on come before the courts in such a shape that the judges, assisted by intelligent witnesses, are very rarely at a loss to understand the invention.

Patent litigation in this country is not so costly, nor so unsatisfactory, as in England, and this fact may be very largely attributed to the effect of our examining system, in reducing and simplifying the questions coming before the courts. But evils, like in kind if not in degree, attend such litigation here, necessary evils where judges are called amidst other duties to deal with a variety of mechanical subjects, of which it is not to be expected that they have personal knowledge, so that they must arrive at their conclusions by such light as the adverse argument of counsel and testimony of experts may throw on the matter.

There is, perhaps, more patent litigation in this country than in England, as there are also very many more patents, the annual number of patents granted being not less than five times more numerous. But it may be gathered from the testimony of Mr. Nasmyth and of others, that in England patent litigation is governed not at all by the number of patents, but by the wealth and courage of patentees. There is likely to be little litigation when it is so expensive as to task the purse of a rich man, and so uncertain that both poor and rich are likely to prefer quiet submission to injustice rather than resort to the courts. It is the characteristic of the English patent system, to the known evils of which the sage newspaper article we have quoted would have us flee from the imaginary evils of our own, that in leaving the validity of a patent, as a title-deed, an open question upon which litigation alone can throw any light, it makes litigation so terrible an ordeal, that sooner than invite it, most ordinary mortals would be content to have their rights remain forever undefined and unrespected.

We fancy the most inveterate and unreasonable grumblers would regard an exchange of our own for this system as a jump out of the frying-pan into the fire.

Patent litigation must always, from the very nature of the subject, be costly; the least that can be done then, in justice to inventors, is to insure that they may enter upon it, when necessary, with a tolerable degree of confidence and certainty, that they have something to stand upon.

One of the remedies proposed by those who understand the subject best, for the present state of patent property in England, is the establishment of special tribunals for the trial of patent causes, in which the judges shall have the assistance of impartial experts upon practical subjects. This, perhaps, is something which might be considered to advantage here. It certainly holds out the prospect of giving patentees the benefit of the most intelligent and satisfactory adjudication of their rights.

But this is only a secondary matter. Among inventors and their advisers there must be many who will be disposed, in drawing up descriptions and claims, to adopt the maxim that "language was made for the concealment of thought," and this tendency must be aggravated if patents are so loosely granted, and there is such uncertainty and risk attending them as to lead to a general impression that vagueness and generality of language may be of service in furnishing some ground, however small, to stand upon. In this way patents become an abomination and a snare, both to inventors and to the public.

Such has been the experience in England; the result of allowing patents to issue without proper examination, *without ascertaining whether the specifications and claims be clear, precise, and well defined*, is thus graphically stated by Mr. Aston: "Patentees complain that they have not sufficient protection for their property, and the public complain that they cannot defend themselves from the patent. There are some intelligent patent agents; there are also some who are not so. It is very commonly the case that an uninformed man goes with his invention to an uninformed patent agent for assistance; the patentee in the latter case is frequently tempted to put in a very wide claim, or one capable of a very wide interpretation. He, therefore, does not as a rule find out the real value of his title-deed till he goes into court with it; *there, for the first time, it undergoes strict examination by the judge on the bench, which is an ordeal which very few specifications can stand.*"

All this gives point to what we have said in the preceding chapter as to the important beneficial effects of our previous examination in compelling clearness and precision in the drawing of specifications and claims.

To overcome these evils, Mr. Aston suggested that there should be an official examination of the document which constitutes the title-deed; he thought that the examiner should be *a lawyer, assisted by persons with technical knowledge.*

Mr. Webster, an eminent Queen's counsel, says, alluding to the duties which the law officers of the Crown under the present system, are called upon to perform: "The law officers do not obtain a sufficient description of the nature of inventions in practice; they are not competent to deal with such subjects; they cannot give the requisite time, and they know nothing about mechanical details. A law officer is the very worst person to discharge the duties for which he is appointed." The act of 1852 made it optional whether they should call in scientific aid, but generally he believed, they call in no such aid. *Every application for a patent should be examined by some one competent person who thoroughly understands the subject of the patent.* If an invention had been patented before, the applicant for the patent should be informed of it.

In a Parliamentary debate on the subject, Mr. Carr, M. P., said, "his impression was that at the root of all the mischief of the present patent law *lay the want of a proper tribunal, the members of which, combining legal and special knowledge, should refuse patents which ought to be refused.*"

Another member of Parliament stated his belief that "if the patent laws were to be maintained, it was necessary that there should be, in the first place, *an examination to ascertain that the invention was new, that it was sufficiently described, and that it was useful.*"

Still another well-known Queen's counsel, Mr. Grove, stated that "he was in favor of the establishment of a special patent tribunal armed with the power of granting or refusing patents on the ground that they are or are not for novel inventions."

Other important evidence to like effect might be cited, but we have given enough to show that among those learned and experienced Englishmen who have given their attention to patent law reform, there is a singular unanimity in the belief that *discrimination* in the *grant* of patents is of vital necessity, and it may be noted that those are the most urgent in advancing this theory who have had opportunity for practical observation of the exercising of such discrimination in our own country.

We see the evils of the want of such discrimination forcibly represented: patents granted with vague and indefinite specifications and claims; patents for old or for useless things, and for things already patented; patentees left to ascertain in the courts the nature and extent of their rights, and yet afraid to resort to the courts, so that both patentees and public are left in doubt and perplexity as to what the majority of patents are for, whether they cover much ground or little, whether they are valid or worthless.

Surely such a state of affairs as this is infinitely worse and more unbearable than any evils which have been or can be engendered by our examining system.

One of the most prominent objections advanced in England to the adoption of an examining system analogous to our own is the demand which the system is supposed to require for highly *scientific officers*, and the supposition prevails here to some extent that the officers of our own Patent Office are or should be *highly scientific men*, and not unfrequently positions in that Bureau are sought on the strength of no other qualification than an assumption of philosophical knowledge acquired by cramming at our schools and colleges.

We cannot conceive a more disastrous event than the filling of our Patent Office with quasi philosophers.

Forty-nine fiftieths of all the applications for patents are based on absolute facts, to be best dealt with practically by matter-of-fact men, who can bring to bear good general and practical knowledge, and powers of discrimination and concentration, without being biased by pet theories of their own.

Purely theoretical knowledge acquired apart from practice is treacherous, and standing alone is but poor capital for an officer of the Patent Office. There have not been wanting instances of theoretical examiners declaring machines and apparatus to be inoperative and impracticable which have been shown to be in every-day successful operation. Whatever science or skill may have been exercised in the production of an invention, the application for a patent goes before the Office, or rather should do, in a dry matter-of-fact condition, and may be better examined by a man of shrewdness, tact, and practical knowledge, than by one who can only bring theoretical lore to bear on the duty. Few theorists think alike, and their efforts to elucidate a simple subject often result in confusing it, precisely as scientific experts in poisoning cases, and in not a few patent cases, by their opposite views, frequently succeed in confusing judges and juries, and in obscuring the truth.

There are classes of inventions which demand from the Examiner a degree of scientific knowledge, but the more practical experience this knowledge may be combined with the better will the duties be performed.

We cannot but think that the alarm in England concerning the difficulty of obtaining efficient officers wherewith to carry out an examining system is a false alarm.

To say that an examining system gives discretion to officials, which good ones may abuse through error or mistake of judgment, and which bad ones will abuse deliberately, is merely to say what is equally true of any system of legal administration depending to any extent upon the discretion of man. If we are to abolish any system in which official discretion is exercised, because good men are not infallible and bad men will do mischief, what branch of government can we permit to survive? To apply such an argument to the examining system is to say that a system proper in its theory and beneficial in its aim is bad for the want of capable and honest men to carry it out, an argument to which we think few of our readers will be willing to subscribe.

We have shown that the discretionary power which the examining system does confer on those who carry it out, is so limited and well-defined that if placed in the hands that the law intended it should be, the chances of injurious abuses of it are small indeed.

We have shown how beneficial the system has been, even admitting it to have been but imperfectly administered, how grossly its defects have been, from natural causes, exaggerated, wherein the real defects lay, and what kind of changes will be likely to remove those defects.

We have brought proof, too, of the evils ensuing from the lack of such a system.

We believe that our readers, candidly weighing all sides of the question, will coincide with us in the belief that the examining system whatever may have been the defects of administration, has been, upon the whole, of incalculable benefit both to inventors and the public, that its abolition would be a great misfortune, a signal for the reduction of patent property to a state of confusion, and that earnest endeavors to improve the organization of the Patent Office, in those respects wherein it very evidently may be improved, will do much to make the system as successful in practice as it is beneficent and just in theory.

CHAPTER X.

REMEDIES FOR DEFECTIVE PATENTS.

HAVING in the preceding chapters discussed as fully as our proposed limits will allow, the examining system, peculiar in its character and intent to our law, we will now turn attention to other provisions, which will be found to be equally endued with the spirit of justice and liberality to inventors.

With a patent granted to him after an inquiry into the novelty and utility of the invention claimed, the patentee may come before the public with a reasonable confidence that his title-deed is clear and distinct, and should infringements upon his patent oblige him to resort to a court of justice, he will in doing so, have the legal and moral benefit of a *primâ facie* presumption of the validity of the right he seeks to vindicate.

Inventors have at times erroneously supposed that the grant of a patent after the examination as to novelty and utility is conclusive upon those questions, and that a patent is a guarantee of the novelty and utility of the invention claimed therein. This, of course, is a mistake. An application for a patent is an *ex parte* proceeding, of which the public at large know nothing. That this should be so, is essential for the protection of the interests of inventors. If before the grant of a patent, the particulars of any claim of invention should be allowed to become matter of public notoriety, very mischievous consequences would be likely to follow.

There are never wanting unscrupulous and narrow-minded men, who if allowed the opportunity would exercise all means in their power to impede and harass inventors and hinder them from attaining their rights. To publish applications for patents would be to invite conspiracy and factious opposition of all kinds from interested parties, with results injurious not only to inventors, but to the peace and morals of society.

It is requisite, therefore, to provide that no claim of invention shall be published prior to the grant of a patent: till then the only parties cognizant of the claim are, *as a rule*, the applicant and his attorney, if he have one, and the Patent Office.

But it is an inviolable maxim that the rights of individuals cannot be bound by proceedings to which the individuals affected were not a party.

Hence the members of the public at large cannot be bound by those proceedings in the Patent Office relative to applications for patents, of which the law does not permit them to know, or to become parties therein. Any member of the public, therefore, is at liberty to show by proper proof, if he can, in legal proceedings upon a patent, that the invention claimed therein was not new or original with the patentee; that it is not useful, or that for other reason the patent should not have been granted, or is invalid.

The patent is *primâ facie* evidence in any suit, for the patentee, this far: that the officials authorized by law have after due examination granted the patent, as for a new and useful invention, which the patentee has sworn that he believes to be his own, and which, in the opinion of these officials, he has clearly and sufficiently set forth and claimed in his specification.

But it may very well be that the patentee was mistaken in his belief that the invention was original with himself, or that he may have taken a false oath, and it may also be that members of the public whose rights the patent may affect, can by facts and proof which were not before the Patent Office, show that such was the case, or that the invention is not useful, or that it is not so clearly and sufficiently described as to enable those skilled in the art to which the invention appertains, or with which it is most nearly connected, to make use of it, from the information which the specification conveys. Any of these defences—as well as others which it is not to our purpose here to speak of, since they are fitter subjects for a legal than for a practical treatise—any member of the public is at liberty to make in a suit which a patentee may bring against him for infringement of the patent. The burden is upon him, however, to establish any of such defences by clear and unmistakable proof, in order to overcome the weight of the *primâ facie* presumption which the existence of a patent raises in favor of the holder.

Mere *technical* defences against patents are not favored, but the courts will always so construe specifications and claims that if possible the patent may stand.

While, therefore, a patent is not to be taken as in any sense a *guarantee* of the patentee's rights, but on the contrary, any member of the public sued for alleged infringement of a patent is at full liberty to show, if he can, that the patent should not have been granted, and that therefore, the grant of it conferred no lawful right upon the patentee, the latter may be sure that he will not have to contend against *hostile* judicial criticism which would give a favorable ear to those technical pleas to which dishonest defendants will be likely to resort.

But though the tendency of our courts is to deal in a liberal spirit with the rights of patentees, this liberality of course cannot extend so far as to give effect to patents palpably deficient in respect to any of the legal requirements. Litigation not unfrequently has the effect of showing the patentee that his patent is defective in some material particular; and that, therefore, his right under it is not such as a court of justice can maintain and enforce. If this defect lie in total lack of novelty or utility in the invention claimed, it is of course beyond remedy. But it may be that the defect consists in the lack of one of these requisites in some part only of the thing claimed, or merely in the mode in which the invention is described or claimed. In its liberal dealings with the rights of patentees, whose patents are thus only partially or technically defective, our law is distinguished from that of any other country.

Under the English law, in a suit for infringement of a patent, proof that the patent includes more than was new and original with the patentee, is altogether fatal to the suit.

Our statutes, however, provide (section 60) that if, through inadvertence, accident, or mistake, and without any wilful default, or intent to defraud, or mislead the public, a patentee shall have claimed in his specification to be the original and first inventor or discoverer of any material or substantial part of the thing patented, of which he was *not* so, he or his legal representative *may yet maintain suit at law or in equity for the infringement of any part thereof which was bonâ fide* his own, provided it shall be a material and substantial part of the thing patented, and be definitely distinguishable from the parts claimed without right, notwithstanding the specification may embrace more than that of which the patentee was the original or first inventor or discoverer.

It will be noted that a patent which is too broad cannot under this section be partially effective, unless upon the face of the patent as it stands the old and the new matter be clearly distinguishable and separable, and the new matter be a material and substantial part of the thing patented. If the old and new matter are not thus definitely distinguishable, the patent as it stands is altogether bad, and no suit can be maintained upon it; but such a state of affairs is not fatal to the inventor's right: he may remedy the error in a mode which we shall allude to hereafter.

The provision in favor of patentees in the section we have quoted is very properly coupled with the condition that in such case no costs shall be recovered in the suit, unless the proper disclaimer has been entered at the Patent Office before the commencement of the suit; nor shall the patentee be entitled to the benefit of the section if he shall have unreasonably neglected or delayed to enter said disclaimer.

This proviso is to protect the public against the carelessness or bad faith of patentees, who might wittingly mislead and deceive the public by continuing to claim that which they themselves were aware they had no right to claim.

It is the right of the public that no patent should purport to grant to the patentee more than he is fairly entitled to. The true extent of his right should distinctly appear on the face of his patent, that the public may be informed of it.

When, therefore, a patentee shall have discovered that his claims include more than that of which he was actual first inventor, he acts in bad faith towards the public, from whom he holds his patent, if he delays to rectify the error, and reduce his claim to its legitimate extent; and much more does he act in bad faith if, with such knowledge, he attempts to enforce submission to his unjust claim by proceedings in the courts.

When, therefore, a patentee discovers that his patent covers more than that of which he was the actual first inventor, and finds that the old matter is definitely distinguishable and separable from the new, he is morally bound to avail himself without delay of the section of the law which permits him to remedy such an error by filing in the Patent Office what is termed a

Disclaimer.

This is a statement in writing, signed by the party disclaiming, attested by one or more witnesses, and recorded in the Patent Office, making disclaimer of such parts of the thing patented as the party in interest shall not choose to claim or hold by virtue of the patent. The right to file a disclaimer is not confined to the patentee, but his heirs or his assigns, whether of the whole or of a sectional interest in the patent, have the like right. Of course, when the assignee of a sectional interest makes such a disclaimer, his interest only is affected by it.

But it is not every patent which is too broad that can be thus cured. The remedy of disclaimer is of course applicable only to cases where the patent specifies and claims *divisible* features of invention. The part retained and the part disclaimed must be clearly separable and distinguishable, and the part to be retained must be a material and substantial part of the thing originally patented.

When, therefore, the patent is not thus divisible, when the original claim is not of such character as to allow of a correction of the patentee's error by cutting out some clearly separable part, the removal of which will yet leave in the patent a material and substantial patentable subject of claim, the remedy of disclaimer cannot be resorted to.

Now there are very many patents inadvertently made too broad, in which the character of the invention, or of the description or claim, would prevent any such rectification of the patent by mere excision. In such case the patentees would be without remedy, and would find themselves deprived of all right without default of their own,—a state of affairs by which very many really meritorious and useful inventors would be irreparably injured.

To obviate such mischief the law has provided the remedy of

Reissue.

This provision is one which has no parallel in any other patent law, and is one of those really beneficent measures which have tended to make our law so effective, because so just and liberal.

Section 53 of the act provides, that "whenever any patent is inoperative or invalid, by reason of a defective or insufficient specification, *or by reason of the patentee claiming as his own invention or discovery more than he had a right to claim as new,* if the error has arisen by inadvertence, accident, or mistake, and without any fraudulent or deceptive intention, the Commissioner shall, on the surrender of such patent, and the payment of the duty required by law, cause a new patent for the same invention, and in accordance with the corrected specifications, to be issued to the patentee, or in the case of his death, or assignment of the whole, or any undivided part of the original patent to his executors, administrators, or assigns, *for the unexpired part of the term of the original patent, the surrender of which shall take effect upon the issue of the amended patent.*"

For patents which are too broad the remedy of reissue is applicable, when the defect is such as to render the original patent altogether inoperative or invalid, because the character of the invention, or of the description and claim is such that there is *no* material or substantial part of the thing patented, which being truly and justly the patentee's own, is clearly separable and distinguishable in the patent as it stands from that which is *not* the patentee's own. In other words, the remedy of reissue is applicable when that of disclaimer is not.

A patent which being too broad may yet be remedied by disclaimer, is not in its original condition altogether inoperative and invalid, but, as we have seen, is by the terms of the law valid, for all that which being a material and substantial part of the thing patented is truly and justly the patentee's own.

Upon such a patent, and for the infringement of such material and substantial part thereof as is *bonâ fide* the patentee's own, he is allowed to maintain a suit, because such part is definitely distinguishable and divisible in the patent as it stands from the parts claimed without right, which latter may, therefore, be removed from the patent by simple excision.

But a patent which being too broad must be remedied by surrender and reissue, is inoperative and invalid, and no suit can be maintained upon it, because the old and new matter cannot be separated in the description and claim as they stand; no distinct part can be taken away and still leave a material and substantial part of the thing patented, definitely distinguishable from the parts claimed without right. Division therefore being impossible, and since the patent as it stands, not being so divisible is wholly invalid, the only remedy is reconstruction of the description and claim, and this can be effected by way of surrender and reissue.

But it is not only as a remedy for patents, which, being too broad, cannot be cured by disclaimer, that reissue is available. It is, in fact, a sort of universal medicine—a cure for all the ills that specifications and claims are heir to. The section we have quoted makes the remedy of reissue available *whenever*, through innocent inadvertence, accident, or mistake, a *defective* or *insufficient* specification renders the patent inoperative or invalid.

The importance of this is apparent when it is remembered that the consideration passing from the inventor to the public, for which a patent is granted, is the making and *disclosure* of an invention. The word disclosure argues a full and candid imparting of all the knowledge necessary to enable others to carry the invention into effect as fully and effectually as the inventor himself; otherwise he has not given the consideration required of him, and therefore his patent is not good. Thus, in the words of our law, "the inventor is required to file in the Patent Office a written description of his invention, and of the manner and process of making, constructing, compounding, and using the same, in such clear, full, and concise and exact terms as to enable any person skilled in the art or science to which it appertains, or with which it is most nearly connected, to make, construct, compound, and use the same." A patent, then, is not valid if essential information is omitted, or if anything be so scantily, obscurely, or unintelligibly stated that the whole description taken together is not sufficient to guide those skilled in the art to a correct and beneficial use of the invention. How likely such defects are to exist where an uninformed inventor has attempted to draw his own description, or has employed an incompetent attorney to do it for him, can readily be apprehended. The right of reissue enables a patentee so to correct or amplify his description as that it shall present a fair and faithful performance of his contract with the public, and so his privilege will be saved to him.

Still another end, beneficial to inventors, is served by the power of reissue.

It is essential to the faithful performance by the inventor of his part of the contract between the public and himself that he should clearly and candidly state what it is that he claims to be his invention, so that the public may be fully advised, from his own statement, of the extent of his right; or, as the law has it, he must "particularly point out and distinctly claim the part, improvement, or combination, which he claims as his invention or discovery."

What is termed the specification comprises the description and this necessary claim, which latter is to be construed with reference to the description. The courts, therefore, thus construing the claim, will always, if possible, give it meaning and effect; and meaning and effect the very fullest,—consistent with the patentee's apparent right,—that by the light which the description affords, they can give it. For not only will they endeavor so to construe the patent that it shall stand; but, if possible, so that it shall be effective to protect the whole of the patentee's apparent invention. But, in doing this, they cannot of course go beyond what appears on the face of the patent. Their liberality must be bounded by the actual contents of the specification. By a liberal construction of the whole document together they can give definite significance to an apparently obscure claim, or give wider meaning to an apparently limited claim, than if it were taken by itself its mere language would imply. But they cannot supply omissions, or construe the patent to cover that which is not directly or indirectly claimed.

Now it may happen, and frequently does happen, that an inventor inadvertently omits such reference in his description or claim to some material and substantial part of his invention as would warrant a judicial construction of his patent as covering that part. This then is a case where the patent, by reason of a defective and insufficient specification, is inoperative to give an exclusive right to the *actual* invention. In such event the patentee may surrender his patent and take a new, or as it is termed, a reissue patent upon an amended specification, which shall distinctly specify and claim the whole of the actual invention *shown*, but not claimed in the original patent.

Again it sometimes happens that one patent has been made to embrace several *distinct* patentable improvements, each of which might have been made the subject of a distinct patent, and it may become proper and desirable thus to separate them. For this the law provides that the Commissioner may in his discretion cause *several* patents to be issued for *distinct* and *separate parts* of the thing patented, upon demand of the applicant, and the payment of the required fee for a reissue, *for each* of such reissued letters-patent.

It is carefully to be borne in mind that the legitimate object of a reissue is simply to correct that wherein the original patent was defective, more fully or correctly to describe or claim the whole of that invention which the original patent should have described or claimed. The words of the law are that the Commissioner shall, on the surrender of a patent, and payment of the required duty, cause a new patent for the *same* invention, and in accordance with the corrected specifications, to be issued; and it is distinctly provided that no *new matter* shall be introduced into the specification. This term, new matter, has reference not to mere language, but to substance. Such changes or amplifications of language may be made as are necessary to effect the legitimate object, the correction of that wherein the original patent was defective, whether in description, or in claim. But no new or changed feature of invention can be introduced, because the reissue patent is to be for the identical thing which constituted the *actual* invention of the patentee *when he applied for his original patent*, and for which that patent would *then* have been granted had the description or claim not been defective or insufficient.

The nature and object of reissues have been greatly misunderstood, and what is intended as a remedial measure in favor of the rights of inventors was, until very recently, oftentimes perverted into a means for unlawfully stretching the apparent scope of patents beyond the true invention, and thus imposing upon and injuring the public.

This was effected, sometimes by basing upon such rudimentary traces of important principles as might be found in a patented invention, broad and sweeping claims couched in language designed, in effect, to cover any known application of such principles to a like purpose, and sometimes by a deliberate interpolation in the amended specification of new matter not to be found in the original patent at all.

Under careless and incompetent administrations this evil practice grew, until it had assumed alarming proportions. No sooner did a patent for some really useful invention become remunerative, and so draw attention, than it became the object of the greedy and unscrupulous to find some old patent worthless in itself, and purchasable for a song, but in which might be found some rude embryonic traces of the principles involved in the valuable patent. Then a reissue was obtained, and all the ingenuity of language was called into play to give this reissue the apparent effect of anticipating and covering whatever was valuable in the later patent. This species of reissue became a weapon wherewith to embarrass and levy blackmail upon meritorious patentees and manufacturers, and either to cut off or compel a division of the hard-earned fruits of their ingenuity, or of their enterprise and invested capital.

This had the effect too of casting a taint of suspicion upon reissues generally, to the great injury of *bonâ fide* meritorious inventors.

It was found necessary to cast some restraints upon the grant of reissues, so as to put a stop to this mischievous practice.

Whereas, therefore, previous to the passage of the last act (July, 1870), reissues might be obtained by the assignees of patents without any reference to the original patentees whatever, it is now required by Sec. 33, that though patents may be reissued to assignees, yet the application must be made, and the new specification *sworn to* by the inventor or discoverer, who may reasonably be supposed to know best what his own actual invention was, and to be the least likely person to make false or rash representations in regard thereto, while the doubt whether the patentee will prove a complacent tool, must tend greatly to check and lessen the speculation which formerly traded in old patents, for no better purpose than the obtaining of brummagem reissues. This provision, however, is not applicable to patents *assigned* previous to July, 1870. This requirement of the law has been somewhat complained of, on the ground that it places assignees of patents too much at the mercy of patentees, and enables the latter, should they be so disposed, to levy blackmail upon those who have already paid them for the property, the title to which it may be found necessary to better by reissue. There may be some ground for this, but the apprehended evil seems to be one which the exercise of proper discretion and care will prevent. More caution than was formerly exercised by purchasers of patents will certainly be required under the present state of the law : this, however, is a material advantage, for the caution required of purchasers must necessarily reflect itself in greater caution upon the part of patentees in the mode of obtaining their patents, since imperfect patents will be found less available commercially.

The same causes (the creation of a spirit of inquiry and discrimination as to patents) which will check the trading in patents for mere speculative purposes, will ultimately serve to check, to some extent, at least, the practices of that class of men, who, under too lax a state of the law, undeservedly flourish, and who may be termed professional patentees; men who, without any merit as inventors, find in small patents a ready means of supplying their pockets, at the expense of the public. While it would be impolitic and wrong to make any distinctions as regards title to the benefit of the patent law, between inventions of different degrees of apparent importance, it is both politic and right to establish any measures which will be likely to raise the general standard of patents in point of *legal* value. This is not more to the interests of the public, than it is to the true interest of *bonâ fide* inventors. Any measure, therefore, which, while it does not tend to work any real hardship to patentees or patent owners, yet tends to impress upon inventors the necessity in their own interest of exercising circumspection in drawing their specifications, is beneficial, and as such a measure may this touching reissues be regarded.

When the patent has been assigned, and there are several assignees, they must all be assenting parties to an application for a reissue.

It is also distinctly specified by the letter of the last act that "no new matter shall be introduced into the specification ; nor in case of a machine patent shall the model or drawings be amended, except each by the other."

This proviso, however, is added : "But, where there is neither model nor drawing, amendments may be made, upon proof satisfactory to the Commissioner that such new matter or amendment was a part of the original invention, and was omitted from the specification by inadvertence, accident, or mistake, as aforesaid."

The wisdom of this last provision, or of the admission under any circumstances of *extrinsic* evidence in applications for reissue, may be doubted. *Bonâ fide* cases for the exercise of this rather sweeping discretion by the Commissioner, must be comparatively very rare, and the measure might seem fairly obnoxious to the charge of extending temptation for much misrepresentation and imposition, without the likelihood of working any very material measure of justice.

As a further necessary check upon the grant of reissues, the law requires that applications therefor shall be subject to revision and restriction, *in the same manner as original applications are.*

As the *surrender* of an original patent does not take effect until the *issue* of the amended patent, if application for the latter be refused and withdrawn, the original remains in force.

It is provided that a reissue patent, with its corrected specification, shall have the effect and operation in law, on the trial of all actions for causes *thereafter* arising, as though the same had been originally filed in such corrected form. Of causes of action under the *original* patent, the surrender and reissue, since it involves a distinct avowal by the patentee that such original patent was inoperative and invalid, is of course an abandonment.

CHAPTER XI.

GENERAL FEATURES OF THE UNITED STATES PATENT LAWS.

IN this, our concluding chapter, we shall refer briefly to those provisions of our patent law which in the preceding chapter have escaped notice.

It is, perhaps, one of the most striking illustrations of the difference in spirit and principle between our patent law and that of England, that whereas in the latter the patentee's right rests upon his being first to disclose the invention to the public *by his patent*, with us the question of right is determined by reference to the date of invention. The inquiry is, who first made, not who first disclosed to the public, an invention which may be in dispute.

Under our law an inventor does not lose his rights merely by public use or sale of his invention during a period *not exceeding two years* prior to his application for a patent. It may be questioned, perhaps, whether this two years grace be not too great a stretch of liberality; certainly, however, it allows time, which in most cases would be ample either for ascertaining practically the positive and relative utility of an idea, or for obtaining that pecuniary aid which a poor inventor may need for the bringing of his invention into use.

Time taken in conducting experiments with an invention is attended with the risk that the invention may be made by some other person in the meantime, or that the idea may come to the knowledge of some unscrupulous party, who will not hesitate to appropriate and patent as his own, the original conception of another, if it seem likely to prove at all valuable. As applications for patent are secret *ex parte* transactions, such theft might be consummated without the knowledge of the true inventor, until on applying for his patent, he should find another party already in possession of a patent wrongfully obtained. This probability, were there no check upon it, would prevent, by making too hazardous, that expenditure of time, money, and skill, which is necessary to reduce many original inventions to the best practical shape, and would compel the premature patenting of half-hatched ideas. This danger the law cannot entirely obviate, but it has provided some measure of protection to inventors during the time which may be required by them for conducting experiments to mature their ideas.

Section 40 of the act provides that any citizen of the United States who has made a new invention or discovery, and desires further time to mature the same, may file a *caveat* in the secret archives of the Patent Office.

Caveats

Are simply brief descriptions setting forth the design of an invention and its distinguishing characteristics, accompanied by a statement that the caveator who claims the invention as his own, is engaged in taking steps to perfect it, prior to applying for letters-patent. This caveat is filed in the secret archives of the Office, and is accessible only to the officials and the caveator, or such persons as he may duly authorize to have access to it. As a caveat refers to an avowedly *uncompleted* invention, while letters-patent are granted only for one which is complete, no proceedings are taken upon a caveat by the Office, but it remains for the caveator to mature his invention and file his application for a patent within *one* year; which time, however, may be extended from year to year by renewing the caveat. It is common to allude to caveats as affording a temporary security, thus leading many inventors to a mistaken impression that a caveat is a sort of temporary patent. This it is not; a patent being a grant of the exclusive right for a certain period to *make, use,* and *sell a completed* invention, is the act of the public in consideration of the *disclosure* of such completed invention. A caveat is merely the caveator's own act in reference to an *incomplete* invention which he desires to keep *secret* till he has had time to mature it, in order that he may then disclose it and obtain from the public the exclusive right to make, use, and sell it. A caveat, therefore, is, as its name implies, simply a *warning*, notifying the Patent Office that the caveator has made an invention, which he intends to mature and to apply for a patent therefor within one year.

The effect which the law gives to this warning is to make it obligatory upon the Patent Office during one year after the *filing* or the *renewal* of a caveat, to grant no patent for the invention to any other claimant without giving the caveator opportunity to establish his priority of right. To this end, notice is to be given to the caveator of the filing of any interfering application for a patent, without, however, informing him as to the name or whereabouts of the applicant, and he is allowed three months from the time of such notice to complete his invention and file *his* application for a patent. If he fail to do this, he will be considered to have waived his claim, and that of the other applicant will be considered and passed upon without reference to the caveat.

Section 24 of the Patent Act provides, that any person who has invented or discovered any new and useful art, machine, manufacture, or composition of matter, or any new and useful improvement thereof, not *known* or *used* by others in *this* country, and not *patented* or *described in any printed publication* in *this* or *any foreign* country before his invention or discovery thereof, and not in public use or on sale for more than two years prior to his application, unless the same is proved to have been abandoned, may, upon payment of the duty required by law, and other due proceedings had, obtain a patent therefor.

It is first to be noticed in this section that the term "any person" includes citizens and aliens, who in reference to the patent laws stand upon precisely the same footing.

And it may be here stated that an inventor, whether citizen or alien, who may have previously patented his invention in foreign countries, does not thereby prejudice his right to a patent here, provided that the invention has not been introduced into *public* use—by which is meant a use in public—in the United States *for more than two years* prior to his application for the patent, but his patent will expire at the same time with the foreign patent, or if there are several foreign patents, then with that having the *shortest* term, and in no case can the term of a United States patent exceed seventeen years from its date (section 25).

Next comes the recital of patentable subject-matters, and then the recital of conditions essential to the obtaining of a patent, and which of course therefore are essential to the maintenance of a patent which may have been granted.

These conditions are—

1st. That the thing for which a

patent is sought shall not have been *known* or *used* by others *in this country* before the *invention* thereof by the claimant.

The mere knowledge or use of the thing in a *foreign* country will not, of itself, bar or invalidate a patent, and proof of such knowledge or use, except it be in the nature of a *patent, or printed publication*, is not admissible against a patent excepting where it is proposed, by bringing home to the patentee a knowledge thereof, to show that his claim of invention was not a *bonâ fide* claim, and that his patent was obtained by fraudulent representation. As to *what* knowledge or use in *this* country will suffice to bar or invalidate a patent, the rule would seem to be that it must not have been an entirely *secret* knowledge or use, but open so far as to argue accessibility by the public: beyond this it matters not how limited the prior knowledge or use may have been.

2d. That the thing for which a patent is sought shall not, prior to the invention thereof by the applicant, have been *patented* or described in any printed publication in *this* or *any foreign* country.

A prior patent for, or printed publication of, a similar thing is the best possible evidence of want of novelty in an invention, and to this end a *foreign* patent or printed publication is equally effective with a domestic one. In either case it is a record, accessible to the public, of the prior existence of the invention claimed by the applicant or patentee as original with himself. But to bar an application or invalidate a patent, a prior patent or printed publication, whether domestic or foreign, should set forth the invention so clearly and intelligibly, as to enable a competent person skilled in that branch of the arts to which the alleged invention may appertain, to make or use it. Mere vague suggestions of something similar will not suffice.

In the absence, then, of any prior knowledge or use *in this country*, and of any patent or printed publication *in this or any foreign country*, an invention is *new* in the eye of the law, and the inventor has an inchoate right therein which he may perfect and secure by a patent.

He is not bound to apply for a patent within any specified time, nor will delay to do so, for however long a time, *of itself*, there being no other claimant, forfeit his right. The statute, however, points out two ways in which the right may be lost:

1. By public use or sale of the invention for *more* than *two* years prior to application for a patent.

Public use is a use, not *by* the public necessarily, but any use— though it may be only limited—*in* public, so that there may be public knowledge of the thing for more than *two* years.

As public use or sale for less than *two* years is not a bar to a patent, and as within such period an inventor might have made his invention a source of profit to himself by manufacture and sale, or by allowing the use of it to others, it would not be right if under a patent subsequently obtained he could disturb or prohibit the further use of the articles thus previously sold by him, or which he had permitted to be made and used. It is therefore enacted by Section 37 that every person who may have *purchased* of the inventor, or with his knowledge and consent may have constructed, any newly invented or discovered machine, or other patentable article, prior to the application for a patent, or sold or used one so constructed, shall have the right to use, and vend to others to be used, *the specific thing so made or purchased*, without liability therefor.

The terms of this section exclude from its benefit those who may, prior to application for patent, have constructed or applied the invention, in defiance of the inventor's right, or without his assent or knowledge.

2. By abandonment.

An invention may be abandoned *at any time* prior to application for patent. But the law does not favor and will never raise, except in the case of public use or sale for more than two years, a presumption of the abandonment of an invention. Before it will be concluded that an invention has been abandoned, there must be some clearly proven act or expression on the part of the inventor, unmistakably indicating his intention not to claim any exclusive right in the invention, but to allow it to become *public property*, for an invention can be abandoned *only to the public at large*.

As a rule, therefore, a *valid* patent may be obtained for any improvement which has not been known or used by others *in this country*, nor been patented or described in any printed publication *in this or any foreign country* before the date of its invention or discovery by the party claiming it as his own, unless he has allowed it to be in public use or on sale for *more than two years* before his application for a patent, or has *at any time* before such application by a voluntary and deliberate act abandoned it to the public.

Should the claim of an applicant for a patent be rejected, or should a patent granted be assailed in litigation, on the ground of a prior foreign patent or description in a foreign printed publication, if the applicant or patentee can establish by competent proof that his invention preceded the date of such prior foreign patent or publication, a patent will be granted him if he be an applicant; or, if he be a patentee, his patent will be sustained.

And, in the case of an applicant for a patent, *ex parte* evidence in such case suffices to establish his priority of right.

Such evidence is also competent to overcome the rejection of a claim for a patent on the ground of description in a printed publication in this country, or a rejection on the ground that the invention is already in public use or on sale, unless it shall appear that such public use or sale has been for more than *two* years prior to the application for a patent.

But if application for a patent be made for something already *patented* in this country, or which another party is at the same time *seeking* to patent here, it may be necessary in either case to try the question of priority of invention in the Office. This is done by means of what is termed an *interference*— a judicial proceeding in which the rival claimants of the same invention are allowed to present testimony in support of their respective claims, the testimony being taken in the same mode as in a cause in equity, and each party having the right to be present at the examination of, and to cross-examine, his opponent's witnesses. This departure from the general rule, which makes applications for patents altogether *ex parte* proceedings, is necessitated by the circumstances of the case. The Patent Office can lawfully grant a patent only to the true and first inventor, and can lawfully grant a *second* patent for the same thing only to him who shall appear to be the actual true and first inventor, and therefore to have a claim superior to that of the first patentee. If, therefore, there be before the Office at the same time two or more parties, each claiming to be the true and first inventor of the same thing; or, if application be made for a patent for the same thing, in which another party already has, by patent granted, a vested exclusive right, testimony must be adduced and proceedings had to determine the question of priority of invention. To these proceedings it is absolutely necessary that the rival applicants in the one case, or the applicant and prior patentee in the other, should both be made parties; for by these proceedings their respective rights *in* the Patent Office are to be bound; and no man's rights are to be bound except by proceedings to which he is a party.

It is provided, therefore, by Section 42 of the Patent Act, that "whenever an application for a patent which, in the opinion of the Commissioner, would interfere with any pending application, or with any unexpired patent, *he shall give notice to* the applicants, or applicant and patentee, as the case may be, and shall direct the primary examiner to proceed to determine the question of priority of invention. And the Commissioner may issue a patent to the party who shall be adjudged the prior inventor."

Some years ago, the proceedings in interference cases were very loose and unsatisfactory. There was no mode of compelling the attendance of necessary witnesses; there was no system or order as to the time and mode of taking the testimony, and the parties were left to develop by such evidence as they could, such a case as they might choose. Consequently, the endeavor of each party was to make out his own case, by the light of that made out by his opponent; and there was every opportunity and temptation to the parties to adapt their proof to the emergencies of the occasion, rather than to the true facts of the case. It can hardly be doubted that the result must have been much injustice, and not a little false swearing.

Judicious improvements, however, in the law, and in the rules and regulations of the Patent Office, have, by assimilating the proceedings in interference cases as far as possible to those in a court of justice, given them a fair degree of the justice and certainty attending ordinary judicial proceedings.

The law has provided for securing the attendance of necessary witnesses by subpœna.

The rules of the Office have provided for proper system in the taking of testimony, by establishing that in all cases the prior patentee or earliest applicant for patent, shall be deemed *primâ facie* the first inventor, thus putting him in the position of a quasi defendant.

The *later* applicant, therefore, or party complainant, must first take testimony to show the date of his invention, for which purpose a certain limit of time is allowed him, after which, within another set period, the prior patentee or appli-

cant must take the testimony in support of his claim, and after the closing of all such direct testimony *both* parties may take *rebutting* testimony.

This right of rebuttal in both parties is necessary. The position of rival claimants of the same invention has not any real analogy to that of complainant and defendant in a suit, the analogy made by the rules of the Office being altogether artificial, and merely for the sake of convenience and order. To such cases no ordinary rules of pleading are applicable. Each party is, in fact, both plaintiff and defendant; there is, therefore, an equal right, as there may be an equal necessity in each party, to rebut his opponent's direct testimony, and it is convenient and orderly that all the evidence which is merely rebuttal of that of an opponent, shall be separate from the direct testimony adduced for the purpose of establishing a party's own case.

This is especially necessary in view of the circumstances in which many cases of interference originate.

We refer, of course, to those cases of frequent occurrence in which there has been some contact or communication, direct or indirect, between the respective parties, leading to a charge, either on one part, or mutual, of theft of the invention in dispute.

As ordinary rules of pleading are inapplicable to interference cases, and no such previous knowledge and control is, therefore, had of the testimony to be adduced as those rules afford, it is essential to both parties to have the like right to rebut if they can, before the close of the evidence, such points as may be first raised in the opponent's testimony.

But these rules would not of themselves suffice to secure the fair trial and adjudication of cases of interference. Of course the main object of each party to an interference, is to establish a date of invention earlier than that proved by his opponent; and if, as under the old rules, the cases to be proved were left entirely in the dark till developed by the evidence, the party taking evidence last would have the opportunity, which he might not always scorn to use, to adapt his proof to the emergencies of the case.

For a pretty effectual method of stopping such possible sharp practice, the public is indebted to the late Commissioner of Patents, Fisher, who established the following beneficial rule:

Before declaring an interference proper, a preliminary interference will be declared, in which each party, without being informed who the interfering claimant is, will be required to file a statement under oath, giving a detailed history of the invention, describing its original conception, the successive experiments, extent, and character of use, and various forms of embodiment, &c. The statement of each party is to be sealed, and not opened until at an appointed time by the examiner of interferences. If that officer then determines that the respective statements show a case warranting the declaration of an interference, he declares it, and neither of the opposing parties can have access to the statement of the other until the time for filing both has expired.

This rule certainly offers some check upon the subsequent proceedings, some bounds to the testimony to be adduced, by confining the parties to a particular case of their own showing, and by affording a basis for cross-examining an opponent's witnesses.

But the rule is serviceable in another way, as allowing the opportunity of nipping in the bud many interferences, which, if proceeded with, might result in nothing but useless expense.

Thus, it is provided, that if the party upon whom rests the burden of proof—*i. e.*, the *latest* applicant fails to file a statement, or if his statement fails to overcome the *primâ facie* case made by the respective applications—*i. e.*, if the date of *invention* given by the later applicant should not be anterior to the date of *application* by the earlier —or if it shows that he has *abandoned* his invention, or that it has been in public use more than two years before his application, the other party will be entitled to an immediate adjudication of the case upon the record: unless a presumption is created that *his right* to a patent is *affected* by the alleged public use of the invention, in which case the interference may be proceeded with. This latter proviso is necessary because a determination against the right of one man to a patent cannot be made upon the *ex parte* statement of another. A person's *ex parte* sworn statement may be allowed to determine the question of his own right, but not that of the right of another. It is further provided that if the *earlier* applicant fail to file a preliminary statement, he will not be allowed to present any testimony going to prove that he made the invention at a date prior to his application.

The preliminary statements are *not* evidence for the parties making them.

Under the present law and office rules, then, cases of interferences may be regarded as a fair and efficient means of trying and determining questions of priority of invention, and a just ultimate decision may be expected in every case, for parties to such a case have the same rights of appeal from the Examiner to the Board of Examiners in chief, and from that Board to the Commissioner of Patents in person, as in other questions touching the rights of applicants for patents.

As regards the cases in which under the law the Commissioner may declare an interference, they include any and every case in which there may arise adverse claims of invention, whether by reason of two or more contemporary pending applications for patents for inventions altogether or in some material part the same, or by reason of an application for a patent or for a *reissue* with a claim to something claimed or clearly shown in any patent or patents previously granted.

This power may be very beneficially used to check what was at one time a practice as common as it is mischievous, that of reissuing patents for the sole purpose of so extending their claims as to cover some feature of value in patents granted subsequently to those sought to be reissued.

In the case of an interference between an application for a patent and a patent granted, the power of the Commissioner extends only to granting another patent to the applicant, should he appear to have been the actual first and true inventor. He cannot recall or cancel the *prior* patent.

His office is in its nature ministerial, and concerns only the *granting* of patents; and his discretionary, or, what may be termed his quasi-judicial powers, therefore, are confined to the consideration and determination of such questions only as concern the *granting* of patents. His duty is to grant a patent to whomsoever may appear to be the true and first inventor of a patentable subject-matter, and justly entitled under the law to receive a patent therefor. In the execution of this duty it is necessary for him to consider and decide disputed questions of priority of invention; but with that and the grant or refusal of a patent, in accordance with his determination, his duty and power end.

The power of *annulling* or decreeing the invalidity of patents, or other public grants, is one of the chancery powers of the courts of the United States.

Consequently where, through the issue of an interference in the Patent Office, or through accident, there are two or more patents for the same thing, of which only one of course can be valid, the invalidity of the others can be authoritatively ascertained and decreed only by a court of the United States having jurisdiction of such questions.

Under Section 58 of the Patent Act: "Whenever there shall be interfering patents, any person interested in any one of such interfering patents, or in the working of the invention claimed under either of such patents, may have relief against the interfering patentee, and all parties interested under him, by suit in equity against the owners of the interfering patent; and the court having cognizance thereof, on notice to adverse parties and other due proceedings had, may adjudge and declare *either* of the patents void in whole or in part, or inoperative, or invalid in any particular part of the United States according to the interest of the parties in the patent or the invention patented. But no such judgment or adjudication shall affect the right of any person except the parties to the suit and those deriving title under them *subsequent* to the rendition of such judgment."

In the case of an interference in the Patent Office between an application and a prior patent, should the applicant be adjudged the prior inventor, the only measure of justice which the Commissioner has power to perform is, by granting a patent to the applicant, to put him in a position to avail himself, should he desire to do so, of the remedy presented by this section against the prior patentee.

The point to be adjudged in a case of interference is "priority of invention." The general rule is that he is in the eye of the law the first inventor who has first *perfected* and *adapted* the invention to use.

But this rule is subject to the qualification that he who first invents, *i. e.*, mentally originates, shall have the prior right, if *he were using reasonable diligence in adapting and perfecting* the invention. Thus it is made by the statute a defence against a patent, that the patentee had *surreptitiously* or *unjustly* obtained the patent for that which was in fact invented by another, *who was using reasonable diligence in adapting and perfecting the same.*

It has been held that the words

"surreptitiously," or "unjustly," as here used, do not necessarily imply that *bad faith* on the part of the patentee must be shown to make this defence available. But it will be deemed that a patent has been wrongfully obtained, when it is for something which was in fact first *invented* by another than the patentee, if the prior inventor *was at the time* using reasonable diligence in adapting and perfecting the invention.

This reconciles the reference in our patent law of the doctrine that "he who is prior in time has the better right" to the time of the making of an invention, with the general maxim that "the laws serve the diligent, and not the slothful." A right of *priority* must be perfected by *diligence*.

The courts will not allow the plea of "prior invention" to overcome the title of a patentee whose patent was obtained in *good faith*, unless it be shown that the alleged prior inventor had actually reduced his conception to practice in a practically useful and operative form, or that being the first to invent, he was, *at the time the patentee obtained his patent*, exercising reasonable diligence to adapt and perfect the invention.

A mere prior conception of an idea, ending in experiment, and never reduced to that practical shape in which alone it can be useful to the public, and can attract public attention, will not suffice to destroy the title of a patentee, who being himself a *bonâ fide* original inventor, has reduced the invention to successful practice, and published it by obtaining his patent.

By these judicially established principles the Patent Office is guided in determining the questions of "priority of invention," in cases of interference.

If the interference be between the claim of an applicant and that of a patentee, the *prima facie* presumption is in favor of the latter, and the burden is upon the applicant to show that he was the first inventor, and also that he had either actually reduced the invention to a practically operative shape before the interfering patent was obtained, or that at the time it was obtained, he was exercising reasonable diligence to bring it into such shape; and, furthermore, it must appear that the applicant has not *unnecessarily* delayed bringing his claim, but that he has been reasonably diligent, as well in bringing his application as in perfecting his invention. If he cannot show this, the first patent will not be disturbed by the grant of a second

Where the interference is between independent *applicants* for patents, there is not that strength of presumption in favor of either party which the possession of a patent, a vested right, creates: still there is a presumption in favor of the *earliest* applicant, on the reasonable principle that, in the absence of proof to the contrary, the first to seek the benefit of the law must be presumed to have the prior and better right. This presumption goes no further than to require that the later applicant must first prove a date for his invention anterior to the application of his opponent, before the latter need offer proof as to the date of his invention other than that which his application affords.

The general principles applied to the decision of priority, as between applicants for patents, are the same as in other cases. He will, as a rule, be held the first inventor, entitled to the benefit of the law, who being *bonâ fide* an inventor first reduced the invention to a practical form beneficial to the public.

As to the evidence which will suffice to prove invention, the rule would seem to be that the idea must have been so far reduced to practice as to have been illustrated or described in a mode sufficient to enable a person skilled in the art to which the invention may refer, to make or practice it, without calling for the exercise on *his* part of more than the ordinary skill of his trade. Less than this will not evidence a matured, and therefore patentable, invention; such an invention as the law will protect.

It will be seen that the question of "diligence" has a most material bearing upon that of "priority of right in law," and this matter of diligence enters not only into the reduction of an invention to practice, but into the making and prosecution of application for a patent, wherever there is a question of right between independent inventors. Especially is this the case where one or other of the disputants is in possession of a patent obtained *in good faith:* the right of such a patentee will not be disturbed in favor of a slothful inventor, prior in point of conception, but who, after the grant of the patent to his competitor, of which as matter of public record he in common with the rest of the public is presumed to have knowledge, has unnecessarily delayed perfecting and adapting the invention to use, and presenting his claim.

It has been found necessary to spur the diligence of applicants for patents even in cases entirely *ex parte* by providing (Sec. 32) that all applications for patents shall be completed and prepared for examination within two years after the filing of the petition, and in default thereof, or *upon failure of the applicant to prosecute the same within two years after any action therein, of which notice shall have been given* to the applicant, they shall be regarded as abandoned by the parties thereto, unless it be shown to the satisfaction of the Commissioner that such delay was unavoidable.

If an applicant for a patent is not satisfied with the justice of a decision of the Commissioner of Patents, refusing him a patent, he may appeal to the Supreme Court of the

District of Columbia, which may reverse the decision of the Commissioner. By the decision of the court, duly certified to and recorded in the Patent Office, the further proceedings in that office are to be regulated, and if no reasons are found for refusing a patent, beyond those raised and adjudicated in the appeal, the Commissioner is bound by a decision favorable to the applicant to issue a patent. But as the court is to consider the case, *on the evidence produced before the Commissioner,* and its decision is confined to *the points raised in the appeal,* if the Commissioner after such decision finds good reasons, not involved in the appeal, or depending upon new evidence not formerly before him, for still withholding the patent, it is within his discretionary power so to do. In other words, the decision of the court upon appeal, if favorable to the applicant, is not that the Commissioner *shall issue* a patent, but that he shall not withhold it upon the grounds raised in the appeal; and it might seem that as often as the Commissioner may refuse a patent upon *new* grounds, the applicant may appeal to the court. The right of appeal to the Supreme Court of the District of Columbia does not extend to parties in interference.

The remedy of an inventor against what he may consider an unjust refusal of a patent does not end even here.

Section 52 of the act provides that when an application for a patent is refused *for any reason* whatever, either by the Commissioner, or by the Supreme Court of the District of Columbia on appeal from the Commissioner, the applicant may have remedy by bill in equity in a court of the United States having cognizance of such cases under the patent law; and the court upon notice to adverse parties, and other due proceedings had, may adjudge that such applicant is entitled, according to law, to receive a patent for his invention, as specified in his claim, *or for any part thereof,* as the facts in the case may appear.

This remedy by bill in equity is applicable to *all* cases where a patent may have been refused.

If the refusal has been on account of an adverse decision by the Commissioner, in a case of interference, the party in whose favor the Commissioner's decision was rendered is entitled to notice, and to become a party in the proceedings upon the bill. Where there is no opposing party a copy of the bill is to be served on the Commissioner.

Proceedings under this section are not in the nature of an appeal, and are not to be governed by the evidence in the case before the Commissioner, but they are original proceedings, in which such original evidence may be adduced as shall be considered essential to arriving at a just decision.

An adjudication in favor of the applicant authorizes the Commissioner to issue such patent as it shall be decided the applicant is entitled to, upon the applicant filing in the Patent Office a copy of the adjudication, and otherwise complying with the provisions of the law.

It only remains now briefly to inquire as to the modes in which a remedy may be had for the infringement of a patent.

There are two ends which it is generally essential to the interests of a patentee he should have the means of accomplishing by resort to the courts,—a remedy for injury from past infringement, and the prevention of infringement in the future.

Damages for infringement may be had by action at law in the Circuit Courts of the United States, or those District Courts exercising circuit court jurisdiction. And as a check upon deliberate, wrongful infringements, the courts are empowered, "whenever in any such action a verdict is rendered for the plaintiff, to enter judgment thereon for any sum above the amount found by the verdict as the actual damages sustained, according to the circumstances of the case, not exceeding three times the amount of such verdict, together with the costs. But this remedy at law is generally quite inadequate to the needs of patentees, since it does not prevent further infringement by the party sued, and for each new act of infringement fresh suit must be brought. For the purpose of preventing further infringement, it is necessary to resort to proceedings in equity, which may be brought in the same courts. Section 55 of the law empowers the courts, upon bill in equity filed by any party aggrieved, to grant *injunctions* to prevent the violation of any right secured by patent, on such terms as the court may deem reasonable."

Injunctions are either *temporary* or *perpetual*. A temporary injunction is one granted before a final hearing of the cause, and may be granted at the discretion of the court at any time after the filing of the bill, upon motion, of which reasonable previous notice shall have been given to the defendant, accompanied by copies of the affidavits to be read in support of the motion.

A temporary injunction prohibits continuance of the infringement complained of in the bill until the question of the complainant's right under his patent shall have been tried, or until further order of the court. It is a summary proceeding, in order to protect a patentee against the irreparable injury that might ensue to him by an unchecked continuance of infringement during the time necessary for bringing a cause to final hearing.

But as it is a proceeding tending to bind the rights of a defendant, before a fair and full trial has been had, and one which may work great, and, as it may prove, unwarranted injury to the party enjoined, the courts exercise the power with great caution, and only where there has been exclusive possession under the patent for some years, with acquiescence of the public in the patentee's right, or where the patent has been previously judicially sustained after full trial at law or in equity; nor will the power be exercised if the defendant, by affidavits, rebutting and overbearing the weight of those of the complainant, can throw reasonable doubt, on grounds not theretofore adjudicated, upon the patentee's title, or can indicate that he is not a mere wrongdoer, but has a good defence against the action. The court in granting a temporary injunction, may couple with the grant such conditions, either on one or on both sides, as under the circumstances of the case may seem reasonable; or, it may allow the defendant to give security to keep an account of profits from the use of the invention, and this it will do, where it appears from the circumstances that in this way the interests of the patentee will be substantially protected, while an injunction would work disproportionate mischief to the defendant. A temporary injunction will not be granted where it appears that the patentee has not been diligent in seeking his remedy, but has allowed infringement to continue for a considerable period of time without taking steps to prevent it.

A temporary injunction may be dissolved at any time upon motion of the party enjoined, made after reasonable previous notice to the complainant, and supported by affidavits showing good and sufficient reason.

A *perpetual* injunction is one granted upon a decree in favor of the patentee after final hearing upon proofs and argument in equity, or after a judgment in favor of the patentee in a trial at law, and its effect is to enjoin the defendant from infringement during the term of the patent.

Formerly it was the practice here, as it still is in England, for the court in equity, when an application for an injunction raised disputed questions of fact affecting the patentee's title, to order a trial at law, that these questions of fact might be passed upon by a jury; but here, since patent causes, whether in law or in equity, are cognizable in the same court, and since it is competent for the court in equity to consider and determine all disputed points in such causes, whether of fact or of law, generally patent cases are now so tried and determined, upon proofs taken after the course in equity, before an examiner appointed by the court.

The questions of fact arising in patent causes are generally of such a nature that they may be determined much more speedily, readily, and satisfactorily by a judge than by a jury, and under the present law all the remedies which proceedings at law might afford a patentee for infringement of his right, he can obtain by proceedings in equity, while the latter will also afford him further remedy, very much more complete and beneficial than he could possibly obtain by proceedings at law.

"Upon a decree being rendered for infringement, the complainant shall be entitled to recover, *in addition to* the *profits* to be accounted for by the defendant, *the damages* the complainant has sustained thereby, and the court shall assess the same, or cause the same to be assessed under its direction, and the court shall have the same powers to increase the same, in its discretion, that are given by this act to increase the damages found by verdict in actions upon the case." (Sec. 55.)

It is not necessary to sustain an action for infringement, that the *whole* of the invention patented should have been infringed, but remedy may be had for the infringement of any material or substantial part thereof claimed.

Actions for infringement may be brought in the name of the owner or joint owners of the legal title to the patent throughout the whole of the United States, or within the particular part or portion of the United States in which the action is brought. A licensee cannot bring such an action, except he join with him the party or parties in whom the legal title to the patent is vested within the territory over which the court wherein the action is brought has jurisdiction. Actions for infringement must be brought during the term of the patent, or within six years after its expiry.

CONCLUSION.

At this point we close our brief summary of the general features of the Patent Laws of the United States, and with it the treatise.

As far as was possible, we have ranged the subjects together in such a way as to produce a connected review of the entire ground. Of course, there are many special matters of law and doctrine respecting patents which have not been touched upon, specialties out of place in a pamphlet avowedly devoted to a grouping of information of a merely general character.

As to those subjects which are treated more at length, we venture to express a hope that our endeavors plainly and concisely to illustrate the principles governing property in invention, will not be altogether ineffectual in throwing light upon matters which have heretofore, by so many minds, been but partially and obscurely understood.

H. & C. H.

THE ACT

RELATING TO

PATENTS

AND COPYRIGHTS.

APPROVED JULY 8, 1870.

PRINTED FROM AN OFFICIAL COPY

ESPECIALLY FOR AND PUBLISHED BY

HOWSON & SON,

AT THEIR

United States and European Patent Offices,

FORREST BUILDING,	MARBLE BUILDING,
119 So. Fourth Street,	605 Seventh Street,
PHILADELPHIA.	WASHINGTON, D. C.

PHILADELPHIA:
SHERMAN & CO., PRINTERS.
1872.

AN ACT

To Revise, Consolidate, and Amend the Statutes Relating to Patents and Copyrights.

Be it enacted by the Senate and House of Representatives of the United States of America in Congress assembled, That there shall be attached to the Department of the Interior the office, heretofore established, known as the Patent Office, wherein all records, books, models, drawings, specifications, and other papers and things pertaining to patents, shall be safely kept and preserved.

Sec. 2. *And be it further enacted,* That the officers and employees of said office shall continue to be: one Commissioner of Patents, one Assistant Commissioner, and three examiners-in-chief, to be appointed by the President, by and with the advice and consent of the Senate; one chief clerk, one examiner in charge of interferences, twenty-two principal examiners, twenty-two first-assistant examiners, twenty-two second-assistant examiners, one librarian, one machinist, five clerks of class four, six clerks of class three, fifty clerks of class two, forty-five clerks of class one, and one messenger and purchasing clerk, all of whom shall be appointed by the Secretary of the Interior, upon nomination of the Commissioner of Patents.

Sec. 3. *And be it further enacted,* That the Secretary of the Interior may also appoint, upon like nomination, such additional clerks of classes two and one, and of lower grades, copyists of drawings, female copyists, skilled laborers, laborers, and watchmen, as may be from time to time appropriated for by Congress.

Sec. 4. *And be it further enacted,* That the annual salaries of the officers and employees of the Patent Office shall be as follows:

Of the Commissioner of Patents, four thousand five hundred dollars.

Of the Assistant Commissioner, three thousand dollars.

Of the examiners-in-chief, three thousand dollars each.

Of the chief clerk, two thousand five hundred dollars.

Of the examiner in charge of interferences, two thousand five hundred dollars.

Of the principal examiners, two thousand five hundred dollars each.

Of the first-assistant examiners, one thousand eight hundred dollars each.

Of the second-assistant examiners, one thousand six hundred dollars each.

Of the librarian, one thousand eight hundred dollars.

Of the machinist, one thousand six hundred dollars.

Of the clerks of class four, one thousand eight hundred dollars each.

Of the clerks of class three, one thousand six hundred dollars each.

Of the clerks of class two, one thousand four hundred dollars each.

Of the clerks of class one, one thousand two hundred dollars each.

Of the messenger and purchasing clerk, one thousand dollars.

Of laborers and watchmen, seven hundred and twenty dollars each.

Of the additional clerks, copyists of drawings, female copyists, and skilled laborers, such rates as may be fixed by the acts making appropriations for them.

SEC. 5. *And be it further enacted*, That all officers and employees of the Patent Office shall, before entering upon their duties, make oath or affirmation truly and faithfully to execute the trusts committed to them.

SEC. 6. *And be it further enacted*, That the Commissioner and chief clerk, before entering upon their duties, shall severally give bond, with sureties, to the Treasurer of the United States; the former in the sum of ten thousand dollars, and the latter in the sum of five thousand dollars, conditioned for the faithful discharge of their duties, and that they will render, to the proper officers of the treasury, a true account of all money received by virtue of their office.

Sec. 7. *And be it further enacted,* That it shall be the duty o. the Commissioner, under the direction of the Secretary of the Interior, to superintend or perform all the duties respecting the granting and issuing of patents which herein are, or may hereafter be, by law directed to be done; and he shall have charge of all books, records, papers, models, machines, and other things belonging to said office.

Sec. 8. *And be it further enacted,* That the Commissioner may send and receive by mail, free of postage, letters, printed matter, and packages relating to the business of his office, including Patent Office reports.

Sec. 9. *And be it further enacted,* That the Commissioner shall lay before Congress, in the month of January, annually a report, giving a detailed statement of all moneys received for patents, for copies of records or drawings, or from any other source whatever; a detailed statement of all expenditures for contingent and miscellaneous expenses; a list of all patents which were granted during the preceding year, designating under proper heads the subjects of such patents; an alphabetical list of the patentees, with their places of residence; a list of all patents which have been extended during the year; and such other information of the condition of the Patent Office as may be useful to Congress or the public.

Sec. 10. *And be it further enacted,* That the examiners-in-chief shall be persons of competent legal knowledge and scientific ability, whose duty it shall be, on the written petition of the appellant, to revise and determine upon the validity of the adverse decisions of examiners upon applications for patents, and for reissues of patents, and in interference cases; and when required by the Commissioner, they shall hear and report upon claims for extensions, and perform such other like duties as he may assign them.

Sec. 11. *And be it further enacted,* That in case of the death, resignation, absence or sickness of the Commissioner, his duties shall devolve upon the Assistant Commissioner until a successor shall be appointed, or such absence or sickness shall cease.

Sec. 12. *And be it further enacted,* That the Commissioner shall cause a seal to be provided for said office, with such device as the President may approve, with which all records or papers issued from said office, to be used in evidence, shall be authenticated.

Sec. 13. *And be it further enacted,* That the Commissioner shall cause to be classified and arranged in suitable cases, in the rooms and galleries provided for that purpose, the models, specimens of composition, fabrics, manufactures, works of art, and designs, which have been, or shall be deposited in said office: and said rooms and galleries shall be kept open during suitable hours for public inspection.

Sec. 14. *And be it further enacted,* That the Commissioner may restore to the respective applicants, such of the models belonging to rejected applications as he shall not think necessary to be preserved, or he may sell or otherwise dispose of them, after the application has been finally rejected for one year, paying the proceeds into the treasury, as other patent moneys are directed to be paid.

Sec. 15. *And be it further enacted,* That there shall be purchased for the use of said office, a library of such scientific works and periodicals, both foreign and American, as may aid the officers in the discharge of their duties, not exceeding the amount annually appropriated by Congress for that purpose.

Sec. 16. *And be it further enacted,* That all officers and employees of the Patent Office shall be incapable, during the period for which they shall hold their appointments, to acquire or take, directly or indirectly, except by inheritance or bequest, any right or interest in any patent issued by said office.

Sec. 17. *And be it further enacted,* That for gross misconduct the Commissioner may refuse to recognize any person as a patent agent, either generally, or in any particular case; but the reasons for such refusal shall be duly recorded, and be subject to the approval of the Secretary of the Interior.

Sec. 18. *And be it further enacted,* That the Commissioner may require all papers filed in the Patent Office, if not correctly, legibly, and clearly written, to be printed, at the cost of the party filing them.

Sec. 19. *And be it further enacted,* That the Commissioner, subject to the approval of the Secretary of the Interior, may from time to time establish rules and regulations, not inconsistent with law, for the conduct of proceedings in the Patent Office.

Sec. 20. *And be it further enacted*, That the Commissioner may print or cause to be printed, copies of the specifications of all letters-patent, and of the drawings of the same, and copies of the claims of current issues, and copies of such laws, decisions, rules, regulations, and circulars, as may be necessary for the information of the public.

Sec. 21. *And be it further enacted*, That all patents shall be issued in the name of the United States of America, under the seal of the Patent Office, and shall be signed by the Secretary of the Interior, and countersigned by the Commissioner, and they shall be recorded, together with the specification, in said office, in books to be kept for that purpose.

Sec. 22. *And be it further enacted*, That every patent shall contain a short title or description of the invention or discovery, correctly indicating its nature and design, and a grant to the patentee, his heirs or assigns, for the term of seventeen years, of the exclusive right to make, use, and vend the said invention or discovery throughout the United States, and the Territories thereof, referring to the specification for the particulars thereof; and a copy of said specifications and of the drawings shall be annexed to the patent, and be a part thereof.

Sec. 23. *And be it further enacted*, That every patent shall date as of a day not later than six months from the time at which it was passed and allowed, and notice thereof was sent to the applicant or his agent, and if the final fee shall not be paid within that period, the patent shall be withheld.

Sec. 24. *And be it further enacted*, That any person who has invented or discovered any new and useful art, machine, manufacture, or composition of matter, or any new and useful improvement thereof, not known or used by others in this country, and not patented, or described in any printed publication in this or any foreign country, before his invention or discovery thereof, and not in public use, or on sale, for more than two years prior to his application, unless the same is proved to have been abandoned, may, upon payment of the duty required by law, and other due proceedings had, obtain a patent therefor.

SEC. 25. *And be it further enacted,* That no person shall be debarred from receiving a patent for his invention or discovery, nor shall any patent be declared invalid by reason of its having been first patented or caused to be patented in a foreign country; provided the same shall not have been introduced into public use in the United States *for more than two years* prior to the application, and that the patent shall expire at the same time with the foreign patent, or, if there be more than one, at the same time with the one having the shortest term; but in no case shall be in force more than seventeen years.

SEC. 26. *And be it further enacted,* That before any inventor or discoverer shall receive a patent for his invention or discovery, he shall make application therefor, in writing, to the Commissioner, and shall file in the Patent Office a written description of the same, and of the manner and process of making, constructing, compounding, and using it, in such full, clear, concise, and exact terms as to enable any person skilled in the art or science to which it appertains, or with which it is most nearly connected, to make, construct, compound, and use the same; and in case of a machine, he shall explain the principle thereof, and the best mode in which he has contemplated applying that principle so as to distinguish it from other inventions; and he shall particularly point out and distinctly claim the part, improvement, or combination which he claims as his invention or discovery; and said specification and claim shall be signed by the inventor and attested by two witnesses.

SEC. 27. *And be it further enacted,* That when the nature of the case admits of drawings, the applicant shall furnish one copy signed by the inventor or his attorney in fact, and attested by two witnesses, which shall be filed in the Patent Office; and a copy of said drawings to be furnished by the Patent Office, shall be attached to the patent as part of the specification.

SEC. 28. *And be it further enacted,* That when the invention or discovery is of a composition of matter, the applicant, if required by the Commissioner, shall furnish specimens of ingredients and of the composition, sufficient in quantity for the purpose of experiment.

SEC. 29. *And be it further enacted,* That in all cases which admit of representation by model, the applicant, if required by the Commissioner, shall furnish one of convenient size to exhibit advantageously the several parts of his invention or discovery.

Sec. 30. *And be it further enacted*, That the applicant shall make oath or affirmation that he does verily believe himself to be the original and first inventor or discoverer of the art, machine, manufacture, composition, or improvement for which he solicits a patent; that he does not know and does not believe that the same was ever before known or used; and shall state of what country he is a citizen. And said oath or affirmation may be made before any person within the United States authorized by law to administer oaths, or when the applicant resides in a foreign country, before any minister, charge d'affaires, consul, or commercial agent, holding commission under the government of the United States, or before any notary public of the foreign country in which the applicant may be.

Sec. 31. *And be it further enacted*, That on filing of any such application and the payment of the duty required by law, the Commissioner shall cause an examination to be made of the alleged new invention or discovery; and if on such examination it shall appear that the claimant is justly entitled to a patent under the law, and that the same is sufficiently useful and important, the Commissioner shall issue a patent therefor.

Sec. 32. *And be it further enacted*, That all applications for patents shall be completed and prepared for examination within two years after the filing of the petition, and in default thereof, or upon failure of the applicant to prosecute the same within two years after any action therein, of which notice shall have been given to the applicant, they shall be regarded as abandoned by the parties thereto, unless it be shown to the satisfaction of the Commissioner that such delay was unavoidable.

Sec. 33. *And be it further enacted*, That patents may be granted and issued or reissued to the assignee of the inventor, or discoverer, the assignment thereof being first entered of record in the Patent Office; but in such case the application for the patent shall be made and the specification sworn to by the inventor or discoverer; and also, if he be living, in case of an application for reissue.

Sec. 34. *And be it further enacted*, That when any person, having made any new invention or discovery for which a patent might have been granted, dies before a patent is granted, the right of applying for and obtaining the patent shall devolve on his executor or administrator, in trust for the heirs-at-law of the deceased, in case he shall have died intestate; or if he shall have left a will, disposing of the same, then in trust for his devisees, in as full manner and on the same terms and conditions as the same might have been claimed or enjoyed by him in his lifetime; and when the application shall be made by such legal representatives, the oath or affirmation required to be made shall be so varied in form that it can be made by them.

Sec. 35. *And be it further enacted*, That any person who has an interest in an invention or discovery, whether as inventor, discoverer, or assignee, for which a patent was ordered to issue upon the payment of the final fee, but who has failed to make payment thereof within six months from the time at which it was passed and allowed, and notice thereof was sent to the applicant or his agent, shall have a right to make an application for a patent for such invention or discovery the same as in the case of an original application: *Provided*, That the second application be made within two years after the allowance of the original application. But no person shall be held responsible in damages for the manufacture or use of any article or thing for which a patent, as aforesaid, was ordered to issue, prior to the issue thereof: *Provided*, That when an application for a patent has been rejected or withdrawn, prior to the passage of this act, the applicant shall have six months from the date of such passage to renew his application, or to file a new one; and if he omits to do either, his application shall be held to have been abandoned; upon the hearing of such applications abandonment shall be considered as a question of fact.

Sec. 36. *And be it further enacted*, That every patent or any interest therein shall be assignable in law, by an instrument in writing; and the patentee or assigns or legal representative may in like manner, grant and convey an exclusive right under his patent to the whole or any specified part of the United States; and said assignment, grant, or conveyance shall be void as against any subsequent purchaser or mortgagee for a valuable consideration, without notice, unless it is recorded in the Patent Office within three months from the date thereof.

Sec. 37. *And be it further enacted,* That every person who may have purchased of the inventor, or with his knowledge and consent may have constructed, any newly invented or discovered machine, or other patentable article, prior to the application by the inventor or discoverer for a patent, or sold, or used one so constructed, shall have the right to use, and vend to others to be used, the specific thing so made or purchased, without liability therefor.

Sec. 38. *And be it further enacted,* That it shall be the duty of all patentees, and their assigns and legal representatives, and of all persons making or vending any patented article for or under them, to give sufficient notice to the public that the same is patented, either by fixing thereon the word "patented," together with the day and year the patent was granted; or when, from the character of the article, this cannot be done, by fixing to it or to the package wherein one or more of them is inclosed, a label containing the like notice; and in any suit for infringement, by the party failing so to mark, no damage shall be recovered by the plaintiff, except on proof that the defendant was duly notified of the infringement, and continued, after such notice, to make, use, or vend the article so patented.

Sec. 39. *And be it further enacted,* That if any person shall, in any manner, mark upon anything made, used, or sold by him for which he has not obtained a patent, the name or any imitation of the name of any person who has obtained a patent therefor, without the consent of such patentee or his assigns or legal representatives; or shall, in any manner, mark upon or affix to any such patented article the word "patent" or "patentee," or the words "letters-patent," or any word of like import, with intent to imitate or counterfeit the mark or device of the patentee, without having the license or consent of such patentee or his assigns or legal representatives; or shall, in any manner, mark upon or affix to any unpatented article the word "patent," or any word importing that the same is patented, for the purpose of deceiving the public, he shall be liable for every such offence to a penalty of not less than one hundred dollars, with costs; one moiety of said penalty to the person who shall sue for the same, and the other to the use of the United States, to be recovered by suit in any district court of the United States within whose jurisdiction such offence may have been committed.

84

Sec. 40. *And be it further enacted,* That any citizen of the United States, who shall have made any new invention or discovery, and shall desire further time to mature the same, may, on payment of the duty required by law, file in the Patent Office a caveat setting forth the design thereof, and of its distinguishing characteristics, and praying protection of his right until he shall have matured his invention; and such caveat shall be filed in the confidential archives of the office and preserved in secrecy, and shall be operative for the term of one year from the filing thereof, and if application shall be made within the year by any other person for a patent with which such caveat would in any manner interfere, the Commissioner shall deposit the description, specification, drawings, and model of such application in like manner in the confidential archives of the office, and give notice thereof, by mail, to the person filing the caveat, who, if he would avail himself of his caveat, shall file his description, specification, drawings, and model within three months from the time of placing said notice in the post office in Washington, with the usual time required for transmitting it to the caveator added thereto, which time shall be indorsed on the notice. And an alien shall have the privilege herein granted, if he shall have resided in the United States one year next preceding the filing of his caveat, and made oath of his intention to become a citizen.

Sec. 41. *And be it further enacted,* That whenever on examination, any claim for a patent is rejected for any reason whatever, the Commissioner shall notify the applicant thereof, giving him briefly the reasons for such rejection, together with such information and references as may be useful in judging of the propriety of renewing his application or of altering his specification; and if, after receiving such notice, the applicant shall persist in his claim for a patent, with or without altering his specifications, the Commissioner shall order a re-examination of the case.

Sec. 42. *And be it further enacted,* That whenever an application is made for a patent which, in the opinion of the Commissioner, would interfere with any pending application, or with any unexpired patent, he shall give notice thereof to the applicants, or applicant and patentee, as the case may be, and shall direct the primary examiner to proceed to determine the question of priority of invention. And the Commissioner may issue a patent to the party who shall be adjudged the prior inventor, unless the adverse party shall appeal from the decision of the primary examiner, or of the board of examiners-in-chief, as the case may be, within such time, not less than twenty days, as the Commissioner shall prescribe.

SEC. 43. *And be it further enacted,* That the Commissioner may establish rules for taking affidavits and depositions required in cases pending in the Patent Office, and such affidavits and depositions may be taken before any officer authorized by law to take depositions to be used in the courts of the United States, or of the State where the officer resides.

SEC. 44. *And be it further enacted,* That the clerk of any court of the United States, for any district or Territory wherein testimony is to be taken for use in any contested case pending in the Patent Office, shall, upon the application of any party thereto, or his agent or attorney, issue subpœna for any witness residing or being within said district or Territory, commanding him to appear and testify before any officer in said district or Territory authorized to take depositions and affidavits, at any time and place in the subpœna stated; and if any witness, after being duly served with such subpœna, shall neglect or refuse to appear, or after appearing shall refuse to testify, the judge of the court whose clerk issued the subpœna may, on proof of such neglect or refusal, enforce obedience to the process, or punish the disobedience as in other like cases.

SEC. 45. *And be it further enacted,* That every witness duly subpœnaed and in attendance shall be allowed the same fees as are allowed to witnesses attending the courts of the United States, but no witness shall be required to attend at any place more than forty miles from the place where the subpœna is served upon him, nor be deemed guilty of contempt for disobeying such subpœna, unless his fees and travelling expenses in going to, returning from, and one day's attendance at the place of examination, are paid or tendered him at the time of the service of the subpœna; nor for refusing to disclose any secret invention or discovery made or owned by himself.

SEC. 46. *And be it further enacted,* That every applicant for a patent or the reissue of a patent, any of the claims of which have been twice rejected, and every party to an interference, may appeal from the decision of the primary examiner, or of the examiner in charge of interference, in such case, to the board of examiners-in-chief, having once paid the fee for such appeal provided by law.

SEC. 47. *And be it further enacted*, That if such party is dissatisfied with the decision of the examiners-in-chief, he may, on payment of the duty required by law, appeal to the Commissioner in person.

SEC. 48. *And be it further enacted*, That if such party, except a party in interference, is dissatisfied with the decision of the Commissioner, he may appeal to the Supreme Court of the District of Columbia, sitting in banc.

SEC. 49. *And be it further enacted*, That when an appeal is taken to the Supreme Court of the District of Columbia, the appellant shall give notice thereof to the Commissioner, and file in the Patent Office, within such time as the Commissioner shall appoint, his reasons of appeal, specifically set forth in writing.

SEC. 50. *And be it further enacted*, That it shall be the duty of said court, on petition, to hear and determine such appeal, and to revise the decision appealed from in a summary way, on the evidence produced before the Commissioner, at such early and convenient time as the court may appoint, notifying the Commissioner of the time and place of hearing; and the revision shall be confined to the points set forth in the reasons of appeal. And after hearing the case, the court shall return to the Commissioner a certificate of its proceedings and decision, which shall be entered of record in the Patent Office, and govern the further proceedings in the case. But no opinion or decision of the court in any such case shall preclude any person interested from the right to contest the validity of such patent in any court wherein the same may be called in question.

SEC. 51. *And be it further enacted*, That on receiving notice of the time and place of hearing such appeal, the Commissioner shall notify all parties who appear to be interested therein, in such manner as the court may prescribe. The party appealing shall lay before the court certified copies of all the original papers and evidence in the case, and the Commissioner shall furnish it with the grounds of his decision, fully set forth in writing, touching all the points involved by the reasons of appeal. And at the request of any party interested, or of the court, the Commissioner and the examiners may be examined under oath, in explanation of the principles of the machine or other thing for which a patent is demanded.

SEC. 52. *And be it further enacted*, That whenever a patent on application is refused, for any reason whatever, either by the Commissioner or by the Supreme Court of the District of Columbia upon appeal from the Commissioner, the applicant may have remedy by bill in equity; and the court having cognizance thereof, on notice to adverse parties and other due proceedings had, may adjudge that such applicant is entitled, according to law, to receive a patent for his invention, as specified in his claim, or for any part thereof, as the facts in the case may appear. And such adjudication, if it be in favor of the right of the applicant, shall authorize the Commissioner to issue such patent, on the applicant filing in the Patent Office a copy of the adjudication, and otherwise complying with the requisitions of law. And in all cases where there is no opposing party a copy of the bill shall be served on the Commissioner, and all the expenses of the proceeding shall be paid by the applicant, whether the final decision is in his favor or not.

SEC. 53. *And be it further enacted*, That whenever any patent is inoperative or invalid, by reason of a defective or insufficient specification, or by reason of the patentee claiming as his own invention or discovery more than he had a right to claim as new, if the error has arisen by inadvertence, accident, or mistake, and without any fraudulent or deceptive intention, the Commissioner shall, on the surrender of such patent, and the payment of the duty required by law, cause a new patent for the same invention, and in accordance with the corrected specifications, to be issued to the patentee, or, in the case of his death or assignment of the whole or any undivided part of the original patent, to his executors, administrators, or assigns, for the unexpired part of the term of the original patent the surrender of which shall take effect upon the issue of the amended patent; and the Commissioner may, in his discretion, cause several patents to be issued for distinct and separate parts of the thing patented, upon demand of the applicant, and upon payment of the required fee for a reissue for each of such reissued letters-patent. And the specification and claim in every such case shall be subject to revision and restriction, in the same manner as original applications are. And the patent so reissued, together with the corrected specification, shall have the effect and operation in law, on the trial of all actions for causes thereafter arising, as though the same had been originally filed in such corrected form; but no new matter shall be introduced into the specification, nor in case of a machine patent shall the model or drawings be amended except each by the other, but when there is neither model nor drawing, amendments may be made upon proof satisfactory to the Commissioner that such new matter or amendment was a part of the original invention, and was omitted from the specification by inadvertence, accident, or mistake, as aforesaid.

SEC. 54. *And be it further enacted*, That whenever, through inadvertence, accident, or mistake, and without any fraudulent or deceptive intention a patentee has claimed more than that of which he was the original or first inventor or discoverer, his patent shall be valid for all that part which is truly and justly his own, provided the same is a material or substantial part of the thing patented; and any such patentee, his heirs or assigns, whether of the whole or any sectional interest therein, may, on payment of the duty required by law, make disclaimer of such parts of the thing patented as he shall not choose to claim or to hold by virtue of the patent or assignment, stating therein the extent of his interest in such patent; said disclaimer shall be in writing, attested by one or more witnesses, and recorded in the Patent Office, and it shall thereafter be considered as part of the original specification to the extent of the interest possessed by the claimant and by those claiming under him after the record thereof. But no such disclaimer shall affect any action pending at the time of its being filed, except so far as may relate to the question of unreasonable neglect or delay in filing it.

SEC. 55. *And be it further enacted*, That all actions, suits, controversies, and cases arising under the patent laws of the United States shall be originally cognizable, as well in equity as at law, by the Circuit Courts of the United States, or any District Court having the powers and jurisdiction of a Circuit

Court, or by the Supreme Court of the District of Columbia or of any Territory; and the court shall have power, upon bill in equity, filed by any party aggrieved, to grant injunctions according to the course and principles of courts of equity, to prevent the violation of any right secured by patent, on such terms as the court may deem reasonable; and upon a decree being rendered in any such case for an infringement, the complainant shall be entitled to recover in addition to the profits to be accounted for by the defendant, the damages the complainant has sustained thereby, and the court shall assess the same, or cause the same to be assessed under its direction, and the court shall have the same powers to increase the same, in its discretion, that are given by said act to increase the damages found by verdicts in actions upon the case; but all actions shall be brought during the term for which the letters-patent shall be granted or extended, or within six years after the expiration thereof.

Sec. 56. *And be it further enacted*, That a writ of error or appeal to the Supreme Court of the United States shall lie from all judgments and decrees of any Circuit Court, or of any District Court exercising the jurisdiction of a Circuit Court, or of the Supreme Court of the District of Columbia, or of any Territory, in any action, suit, controversy, or case, at law or in equity, touching patent rights, in the same manner and under the same circumstances as in other judgments and decrees of such Circuit Courts, without regard to sum or value in controversy.

Sec. 57. *And be it further enacted*, That written or printed copies of any records, books, papers, or drawings, belonging to the Patent Office, and of letters-patent under the signature of the Commissioner, or acting commissioner, with the seal of office affixed, shall be competent evidence in all cases wherein the originals could be evidence, and any person making application therefor, and paying the fee required by law, shall have certified copies thereof. And copies of the specifications and drawings of foreign letters-patent, of record in the Patent Office, certified in like manner, shall be *prima facie* evidence of the fact of the granting of such foreign letters-patent, and of the date and contents thereof.

Sec. 58. *And be it further enacted*, That whenever there shall be interfering patents, any person interested in any one of such interfering patents, or in the working of the invention claimed under either of such patents, may have relief against the interfering patentee and all parties interested under him by suit in equity against the owners of the interfering patent; and the court having cognizance thereof, as hereinbefore provided, on notice to adverse parties, and other due proceedings had, according to the course of equity, may adjudge and declare either of the patents void in whole or in part, or inoperative, or invalid in any particular part of the United States, according to the interest of the parties in the patent or the invention patented. But no such judgment or adjudication shall affect the rights of any person, except the parties to the suit and those deriving title under them subsequent to the rendition of such judgment.

SEC. 59. *And be it further enacted*, That damages for the infringement of any patent may be recovered by action on the case in any Circuit Court of the United States, or District Court exercising the jurisdiction of a Circuit Court, or in the Supreme Court of the District of Columbia, or of any Territory, in the name of the party interested, either as patentee, assignee, or grantee. And whenever in any such action a verdict shall be rendered for the plaintiff, the Court may enter judgment thereon for any sum above the amount found by the verdict as the actual damages sustained, according to the circumstances of the case, not exceeding three times the amount of such verdict, together with the costs.

SEC. 60. *And be it further enacted*, That whenever, through inadvertence, accident, or mistake, and without any wilful default or intent to defraud or mislead the public, a patentee shall have, in his specification, claimed to be the original and first inventor or discoverer of any material or substantial part of the thing patented, of which he was not the original and first inventor or discoverer, as aforesaid, every such patentee, his executors, administrators, and assigns, whether of the whole or any sectional interest in the patent, may maintain a suit at law or in equity, for the infringement of any part thereof, which was *bona fide* his own, provided it shall be a material and substantial part of the thing patented, and be definitely distinguishable from the parts so claimed, without right as aforesaid, notwithstanding the specifications may embrace more than that of which the patentee was the original or first inventor or discoverer. But in every such case in which a judgment or decree shall be rendered for the plaintiff, no costs shall be recovered, unless the proper disclaimer has been entered at the Patent Office before the commencement of the suit; nor shall he be entitled to the benefits of this section, if he shall have unreasonably neglected or delayed to enter said disclaimer.

SEC. 61. *And be it further enacted,* That in any action for infringement the defendant may plead the general issue, and having given notice in writing to the plaintiff or his attorney, thirty days before, may prove, on trial, any one or more of the following special matters:

First. That for the purpose of deceiving the public the description and specification filed by the patentee in the Patent Office was made to contain less than the whole truth relative to his invention or discovery, or more than is necessary to produce the desired effect; or,

Second. That he had surreptitiously or unjustly obtained the patent for that which was in fact invented by another, who was using reasonable diligence in adapting and perfecting the same; or,

Third. That it had been patented or described in some printed publication prior to his supposed invention or discovery thereof; or,

Fourth. That he was not the original and first inventor or discoverer of any material and substantial part of the thing patented; or,

Fifth. That it had been in public use or on sale in this country, for more than two years before his application for a patent, or had been abandoned to the public.

And in notices as to proof of previous invention, knowledge, or use of the thing patented, the defendant shall state the names of patentees and the dates of their patents, and when granted, and the names and residences of the persons alleged to have invented, or to have had the prior knowledge of the thing patented, and where and by whom it had been used; and if any one or more of the special matters alleged shall be found for the defendant, judgment shall be rendered for him, with costs. And the like defences may be pleaded in any suit in equity for relief against an alleged infringement; and proofs of the same may be given upon like notice in the answer of the defendant, and with the like effect.

Sect. 62. *And be it further enacted*, That whenever it shall appear that the patentee, at the time of making his application for the patent, believed himself to be the original and first inventor or discoverer of the thing patented, the same shall not be held to be void on account of the invention or discovery, or any part thereof, having been known or used in a foreign country, before his invention or discovery thereof, if it had not been patented, or described in a printed publication.

Sec. 63. *And be it further enacted*, That where the patentee of any invention or discovery, the patent for which was granted prior to the second day of March, eighteen hundred and sixty-one, shall desire an extension of his patent beyond the original term of its limitation, he shall make application therefor, in writing, to the Commissioner, setting forth the reasons why such extension should be granted; and he shall also furnish a written statement under oath of the ascertained value of the invention or discovery, and of his receipts and expenditures on account thereof, sufficiently in detail to exhibit a true and faithful account of the loss and profit in any manner accruing to him by reason of said invention or discovery. And said application shall be filed not more than six months nor less than ninety days before the expiration of the original term of the patent, and no extension shall be granted after the expiration of said original term.

Sec. 64. *And be it further enacted*, That upon the receipt of such application, and the payment of the duty required by law, the Commissioner shall cause to be published in one newspaper in the city of Washington, and in such other papers published in the section of the country most interested adversely to the extension of the patent as he may deem proper, for at least sixty days prior to the day set for hearing the case, a notice of such application, and of the time and place when and where the same will be considered, that any person may appear and show cause why the extension should not be granted.

Sec. 65. *And be it further enacted*, That on the publication of such notice, the Commissioner shall refer the case to the principal examiner having charge of the class of inventions to which it belongs, who shall make to said Commissioner a full report of the case, and particularly whether the invention or discovery was new and patentable when the original patent was granted.

SEC. 66. *And be it further enacted,* That the Commissioner shall, at the time and place designated in the published notice, hear and decide upon the evidence produced, both for and against the extension; and if it shall appear to his satisfaction that the patentee, without neglect or fault on his part, has failed to obtain from the use and sale of his invention or discovery a reasonable remuneration for the time, ingenuity, and expense bestowed upon it, and the introduction of it into use, and that it is just and proper, having due regard to the public interest, that the term of the patent should be extended, the said Commissioner shall make a certificate thereon, renewing and extending the said patent for the term of seven years from the expiration of the first term, which certificate shall be recorded in the Patent Office, and thereupon the said patent shall have the same effect in law as though it had been originally granted for twenty-one years.

SEC. 67. *And be it further enacted,* That the benefit of the extension of a patent shall extend to the assignees and grantees of the right to use the thing patented to the extent of their interest therein.

SEC. 68. *And be it further enacted,* That the following shall be the rates for patent fees:

On filing each original application for a patent, fifteen dollars.
On issuing each original patent, twenty dollars.
On filing each caveat, ten dollars.
On every application for the reissue of a patent, thirty dollars.
On filing each disclaimer, ten dollars.
On every application for the extension of a patent, fifty dollars.
On the granting of every extension of a patent, fifty dollars.
On an appeal for the first time from the primary examiners to the examiners-in-chief, ten dollars.
On every appeal from the examiners-in-chief to the Commissioner, twenty dollars.
For certified copies of patents and other papers, ten cents per hundred words.
For recording every assignment, agreement, power of attorney, or other paper, of three hundred words or under, one dollar; of over three hundred and under one thousand words, two dollars; of over one thousand words, three dollars.
For copies of drawings, the reasonable cost of making them.

Sec. 69. *And be it further enacted,* That patent fees may be paid to the Commissioner, or to the Treasurer or any of the assistant treasurers of the United States, or to any of the designated depositaries, national banks, or receivers of public money, designated by the Secretary of the Treasury for that purpose, who shall give the depositor a receipt or certificate of deposit therefor. And all money received at the Patent Office, for any purpose, or from any source whatever, shall be paid into the treasury as received, without any deduction whatever; and all disbursements for said office shall be made by the disbursing clerk of the Interior Department.

Sec. 70. *And be it further enacted,* That the Treasurer of the United States is authorized to pay back any sum or sums of money to any person who shall have paid the same into the treasury, or to any receiver or depositary, to the credit of the Treasurer, as for fees accruing at the Patent Office, through mistake, certificate thereof being made to said Treasurer by the Commissioner of Patents.

PROVISIONS OF THE ACT OF JULY 8TH, 1870, AS TO
DESIGNS.

SEC. 71. *And be it further enacted*, That any person who, by his own industry, genius, efforts, and expense, has invented or produced any new and original design for a manufacture, bust, statue, alto-relievo, or bas-relief; any new and original design for the printing of woollen, silk, cotton, or other fabrics; any new and original impression, ornament, pattern, print, or picture, to be printed, painted, cast, or otherwise placed on or worked into any article of manufacture; or any new, useful, and original shape or configuration of any article of manufacture, the same not having been known or used by others before his invention or production thereof, or patented or described in any printed publication, may, upon payment of the duty required by law, and other due proceedings had the same as in cases of invention or discoveries, obtain a patent therefor.

SEC. 72. *And be it further enacted*, That the Commissioner may dispense with models of designs when the design can be sufficiently represented by drawings or photographs.

SEC. 73. *And be it further enacted*, That patents for designs may be granted for the term of three years and six months, or for seven years, or for fourteen years, as the applicant may in his application elect.

SEC. 74. *And be it further enacted*, That patentees of designs *issued prior to March two, eighteen hundred and sixty-one*, shall be entitled to the extension of their respective patents for the term of seven years, in the same manner and under the same restrictions as are provided for the extension of patents for inventions or discoveries, issued prior to the second day of March, eighteen hundred and sixty-one.

SEC. 75. *And be it further enacted*, That the following shall be the rates of fees in design cases:

For three years and six months, ten dollars.
For seven years, fifteen dollars.
For fourteen years, thirty dollars.
For all other cases in which fees are required, the same rates as in cases of inventions or discoveries.

SEC. 76. *And be it further enacted,* That all the regulations and provisions which apply to the obtaining or protection of patents for inventions or discoveries, not inconsistent with the provisions of this *act,* shall apply to patents for designs.

PROVISIONS OF THE ACT OF JULY 8TH, 1870, AS TO

TRADE-MARKS.

SEC. 77. *And be it further enacted*, That any person or firm domiciled in the United States, and any corporation created by the authority of the United States, or of any State or Territory thereof, and any person, firm, or corporation resident of or located in any foreign country which by treaty or convention affords similar privileges to citizens of the United States, and who are entitled to the exclusive use of any lawful trademark, or who intend to adopt and use any trade-mark for exclusive use within the United States, may obtain protection for such lawful trade-mark by complying with the following requirements, to wit:

First. By causing to be recorded in the Patent Office the names of the parties and their residences and place of business, who desire the protection of the trade-mark.

Second. The class of merchandise and the particular description of goods comprised in such class, by which the trade-mark has been or is intended to be appropriated.

Third. A description of the trade-mark itself, with fac similes thereof, and the mode in which it has been or is intended to be applied and used.

Fourth. The length of time, if any, during which the trademark has been used.

Fifth. The payment of a fee of twenty-five dollars, in the same manner and for the same purpose as the fee required for patents.

Sixth. The compliance with such regulations as may be prescribed by the Commissioner of Patents.

Seventh. The filing of a declaration, under the oath of the person, or of some member of the firm or officer of the corporation, to the effect that the party claiming protection for the trade-mark has a right to the use of the same, and that no other person, firm, or corporation has the right to such use, either in the identical form or having such near resemblance thereto as might be calculated to deceive, and that the description and fac similes presented for record are true copies of the trade-mark sought to be protected.

SEC. 78. *And be it further enacted*, That such trade-mark shall remain in force for thirty years from the date of such registration, except in cases where such trade-mark is claimed for and applied to articles not manufactured in this country and in which it receives protection under the laws of any foreign country for a shorter period, in which case it shall cease to have any force in this country by virtue of this act at the same time that it becomes of no effect elsewhere, and during the period that it remains in force it shall entitle the person, firm, or corporation registering the same to the exclusive use thereof so far as regards the description of goods to which it is appropriated in the statement filed under oath as aforesaid, and no other person shall lawfully use the same trade-mark, or substantially the same, or so nearly resembling it as to be calculated to deceive, upon substantially the same description of goods: *Provided*, That six months prior to the expiration of said term of thirty years, application may be made for a renewal of such registration, under regulations to be prescribed by the Commissioner of Patents, and the fee for such renewal shall be the same as for the original registration; certificate of such renewal shall be issued in the same manner as for the original registration, and such trade-mark shall remain in force for a further term of thirty years: *And provided further*, That nothing in this section shall be construed by any court as abridging or in any manner affecting unfavorably the claim of any person, firm, corporation, or company to any trade-mark after the expiration of the term for which such trade-mark was registered.

SEC. 79. *And be it further enacted*, That any person or corporation who shall reproduce, counterfeit, copy, or imitate any such recorded trade-mark, and affix the same to goods of substantially the same descriptive properties and qualities as those referred to in the registration, shall be liable to an action on the case for damages for such wrongful use of said trade-mark, at the suit of the owner thereof, in any court of competent jurisdiction in the United States, and the party aggrieved shall also have his remedy according to the course of equity to enjoin the wrongful use of his trade-mark and to recover compensation therefor in any court having jurisdiction over the person guilty of such wrongful use. The Commissioner of Patents shall not receive and record any proposed trade-mark which is not and cannot become a lawful trade-mark, or which is merely the name of a person, firm, or corporation only, unaccompanied by a mark sufficient to distinguish it from the same name when used by other persons, or which is identical with a trade-mark appropriate to the same class of merchandise and belonging to a different owner, and already registered or received for registration, or which so nearly resembles such last-mentioned trade-mark as to be likely to deceive the public: *Provided*, That this section shall not prevent the registry of any lawful trade-mark rightfully used at the time of the passage of this act.

Sec. 80. *And be it further enacted*, That the time of the receipt of any trade-mark at the Patent Office for registration shall be noted and recorded, and copies of the trade-mark and of the date of the receipt thereof, and of the statement filed therewith, under the seal of the Patent Office, certified by the Commissioner, shall be evidence in any suit in which such trade-mark shall be brought in controversy.

Sec. 81. *And be it further enacted*, That the Commissioner of Patents is authorized to make rules, regulations, and prescribe forms for the transfer of the right to the use of such trade-marks, conforming as nearly as practicable to the requirements of law respecting the transfer and transmission of copyrights.

Sec. 82. *And be it further enacted*, That any person who shall procure the registry of any trade-mark, or of himself as the owner thereof, or an entry respecting a trade-mark in the Patent Office under this act, by making any false or fraudulent representations or declarations, verbally or in writing, or by any fraudulent means, shall be liable to pay damages in consequence of any such registry or entry to the person injured thereby, to be recovered in an action on the case before any court of competent jurisdiction within the United States.

Sec. 83. *And be it further enacted*, That nothing in this act shall prevent, lessen, impeach, or avoid any remedy at law or in equity, which any party aggrieved by any wrongful use of any trade-mark might have had if this act had not been passed.

Sec. 84. *And be it further enacted*, That no action shall be maintained under the provisions of this act by any person claiming the exclusive right to any trade-mark which is used or claimed in any unlawful business, or upon any article which is injurious in itself, or upon any trade-mark which has been fraudulently obtained, or which has been formed and used with the design of deceiving the public in the purchase or use of any article of merchandise.

PROVISIONS OF THE ACT OF JULY 8TH, 1870, AS TO
COPYRIGHTS.

SEC. 85. *And be it further enacted,* That all records and other things relating to copyrights and required by law to be preserved, shall be under the control of the Librarian of Congress, and kept and preserved in the Library of Congress; and the Librarian of Congress shall have the immediate care and supervision thereof, and, under the supervision of the Joint Committee of Congress on the Library, shall perform all acts and duties required by law touching copyrights. The Librarian shall cause a seal to be provided for said office, with such device as the Joint Committee on the Library may approve, with which all records or papers issued from said office, and to be used in evidence, shall be authenticated. He shall also give an additional bond, with sureties, to the Treasurer of the United States, in the sum of five thousand dollars, with the condition that he will render to the proper officers of the treasury a true account of all moneys received by virtue of his office. He shall also make an annual report to Congress of the number and description of copyright publications for which entries have been made during the year. And the Librarian of Congress shall receive a yearly compensation of four thousand dollars, to commence when this act shall take effect.

SEC. 86. *And be it further enacted,* That any citizen of the United States, or resident therein, who shall be the author, inventor, designer, or proprietor of any book, map, chart, dramatic or musical composition, engraving, cut, print, or photograph or negative thereof, or of a painting, drawing, chromo, statue, statuary, and of models or designs intended to be perfected as works of the fine arts, and his executors, administrators, or assigns, shall, upon complying with the provisions of this act, have the sole liberty of printing, reprinting, publishing, completing, copying, executing, finishing, and vending the same; and in the case of a dramatic composition, of publicly performing or representing it, or causing it to be performed or represented by others; and authors may reserve the right to dramatize or to translate their own works.

SEC. 87. *And be it further enacted,* That copyrights shall be granted for the term of twenty-eight years from the time of recording the title thereof, in the manner hereinafter directed.

Sec. 88. *And be it further enacted,* That the author, inventor, or designer, if he be still living and a citizen of the United States or resident therein, or his widow or children, if he be dead, shall have the same exclusive right continued for the further term of fourteen years, upon recording the title of the work or description of the article so secured a second time, and complying with all other regulations in regard to original copyrights, within six months before the expiration of the first term. And such person shall, within two months from the date of said renewal, cause a copy of the record thereof to be published in one or more newspapers, printed in the United States, for the space of four weeks.

Sec. 89. *And be it further enacted,* That copyrights shall be assignable in law, by any instrument of writing, and such assignment shall be recorded in the office of the Librarian of Congress within sixty days after its execution, in default of which it shall be void as against any subsequent purchaser or mortgagee for a valuable consideration, without notice.

Sec. 90. *And be it further enacted,* That no person shall be entitled to a copyright unless he shall, before publication, deposit in the mail a printed copy of the title of the book or other article, or a description of the painting, drawing, chromo, statue, statuary, or model or design for a work of the fine arts, for which he desires a copyright, addressed to the Librarian of Congress, and, within ten days from the publication thereof, deposit in the mail two copies of such copyright book or other article, or in case of a painting, drawing, statue, statuary, model or design for a work of the fine arts, a photograph of the same, to be addressed to said Librarian of Congress, as hereinafter to be provided.

Sec. 91. *And be it further enacted,* That the Librarian of Congress shall record the name of such copyright book or other article, forthwith in a book to be kept for that purpose, in the words following: " Library of Congress, to wit: Be it remembered that on the ——— day of ———, Anno Domini ———, A. B., of ———, hath deposited in this office the title of a book (map, chart, or otherwise, as the case may be, or description of the article), the title or description of which is in the following words, to wit: (here insert the title or description), the right whereof he claims as author, originator (or proprietor, as the case may be), in conformity with the laws of the United States respecting copyrights. C. D., Librarian of Congress." And he shall give a copy of the title or description, under the seal of the Librarian of Congress, to said proprietor, whenever he shall require it.

SEC. 92. *And be it further enacted,* That for recording the title or description of any copyright book or other article, the Librarian of Congress shall receive, from the person claiming the same, fifty cents; and for every copy under seal actually given to such person or his assigns, fifty cents; and for recording any instrument of writing for the assignment of a copyright, fifteen cents for every one hundred words; and for every copy thereof, ten cents for every one hundred words, which moneys, so received, shall be paid into the Treasury of the United States.

SEC. 93. *And be it further enacted,* That the proprietor of every copyright book or other article shall mail to the Librarian of Congress at Washington, within ten days after its publication, two complete printed copies thereof, of the best edition issued, or description or photograph of such article as hereinbefore required, and a copy of every subsequent edition wherein any substantial changes shall be made.

SEC. 94. *And be it further enacted,* That in default of such deposit in the post-office, said proprietor shall be liable to a penalty of twenty-five dollars, to be collected by the Librarian of Congress, in the name of the United States, in an action of debt in any District Court of the United States, within the jurisdiction of which the delinquent may reside or be found.

SEC. 95. *And be it further enacted,* That any such copyright book or other article may be sent to the Librarian of Congress by mail, free of postage, provided the words "Copyright Matter" are plainly written or printed on the outside of the package containing the same.

SEC. 96. *And be it further enacted,* That the postmaster to whom such copyright book, title, or other article is delivered, shall, if requested, give a receipt therefor; and when so delivered he shall mail it to its destination without cost to the proprietor.

Sec. 97. *And be it further enacted,* That no person shall maintain an action for the infringement of his copyright unless he shall give notice thereof by inserting in the several copies of every edition published, on the title-page or the page immediately following, if it be a book; or if a map, chart, musical composition, print, cut, engraving, photograph, painting, drawing, chromo, statue, statuary, or model or design intended to be perfected and completed as a work of the fine arts, by inscribing upon some portion of the face or front thereof, or on the face of the substance on which the same shall be mounted, the following words, viz.: "Entered according to act of Congress, in the year ——, by A. B., in the office of the Librarian of Congress, at Washington."

Sec. 98. *And be it further enacted,* That if any person shall insert or impress such notice, or words of the same purport, in or upon any book, map, chart, musical composition, print, cut, engraving, or photograph, or other articles herein named, for which he has not obtained a copyright, every person so offending shall forfeit and pay one hundred dollars; one moiety thereof to the person who shall sue for the same, and the other to the use of the United States, to be recovered by action in any court of competent jurisdiction.

Sec. 99. *And be it further enacted,* That if any person, after the recording of the title of any book as herein provided, shall within the term limited, and without the consent of the proprietor of the copyright first obtained in writing, signed in presence of two or more witnesses, print, publish, or import, or, knowing the same to be so printed, published, or imported, shall sell or expose to sale any copy of such book, such offender shall forfeit every copy thereof to said proprietor, and shall also forfeit and pay such damages as may be recovered in a civil action by such proprietor in any court of competent jurisdiction.

Sec. 100. *And be it further enacted,* That if any person, after the recording of the title of any map, chart, musical composition, print, cut, engraving, or photograph, or chromo, or of the description of any painting, drawing, statue, statuary, or model or design intended to be perfected and executed as a work of the fine arts, as herein provided, shall, within the term limited, and without the consent of the proprietor of the copyright first obtained in writing, signed in presence of two or more witnesses, engrave, etch, work, copy, print, publish, or import, either in whole or in part, or by varying the main design with intent to evade the law, or, knowing the same to be so printed, published, or imported, shall sell or expose to sale any copy of such map or other article, as aforesaid, he shall forfeit to the said proprietor all the plates on which the same shall be copied, and every sheet thereof, either copied or printed, and shall further forfeit one dollar for every sheet of the same found in his possession, either printing, printed, copied, published, imported, or exposed for sale; and in case of a painting, statue, or statuary, he shall forfeit ten dollars for every copy of the same in his possession, or which have by him been sold or exposed for sale; one moiety thereof to the proprietor, and the other to the use of the United States, to be recovered by action in any court of competent jurisdiction.

SEC. 101. *And be it further enacted*, That any person publicly performing or representing any dramatic composition for which a copyright has been obtained, without the consent of the proprietor thereof, or his heirs or assigns, shall be liable for damages therefor, to be recovered by action in any court of competent jurisdiction; said damages in all cases to be assessed at such sum, not less than one hundred dollars for the first, and fifty dollars for every subsequent performance, as to the court shall appear to be just.

SEC. 102. *And be it further enacted*, That any person who shall print or publish any manuscript whatever, without the consent of the author or proprietor first obtained (if such author or proprietor be a citizen of the United States, or resident therein), shall be liable to said author or proprietor for all damages occasioned by such injury, to be recovered by action on the case in any court of competent jurisdiction.

SEC. 103. *And be it further enacted*, That nothing herein contained shall be construed to prohibit the printing, publishing, importation, or sale of any book, map, chart, dramatic or musical composition, print, cut, engraving, or photograph, written, composed, or made by any person not a citizen of the United States, nor resident therein.

Sec. 104. *And be it further enacted,* That no action shall be maintained in any case of forfeiture or penalty under the copyright laws, unless the same is commenced within two years after the cause of action has arisen.

Sec. 105. *And be it further enacted,* That in all actions arising under the laws respecting copyrights the defendant may plead the general issue, and give the special matter in evidence.

Sec. 106. *And be it further enacted,* That all actions, suits, controversies, and cases arising under the copyright laws of the United States shall be originally cognizable, as well in equity as at law, whether civil or penal in their nature, by the Circuit Courts of the United States, or any District Court having the jurisdiction of a Circuit Court, or in the Supreme Court of the District of Columbia, or any Territory. And the court shall have power, upon bill in equity, filed by any party aggrieved, to grant injunctions to prevent the violation of any right secured by said laws, according to the course and principles of courts of equity, on such terms as the court may deem reasonable.

Sec. 107. *And be it further enacted,* That a writ of error or appeal to the Supreme Court of the United States shall lie from all judgments and decrees of any court, in any action, suit, controversy, or case touching copyrights, in the same manner and under the same circumstances as in other judgments and decrees of such courts, without regard to the sum or value in controversy.

Sec. 108. *And be it further enacted,* That in all recoveries under the copyright laws, either for damages, forfeitures, or penalties, full costs shall be allowed thereon.

Sec. 109. *And be it further enacted,* That all books, maps, charts, and other publications of every nature whatever, heretofore deposited in the Department of the Interior, according to the laws regulating copyrights, together with all the records of said department, and all records concerning the same which were removed by the Department of the Interior from the Department of State, shall be removed to, and be under the control of the Librarian of Congress, who is hereby charged with all the duties pertaining to copyrights required by law.

Sec. 110. *And be it further enacted,* That the Clerk of each of the District Courts of the United States, shall transmit forthwith to the Librarian of Congress, all books, maps, prints, photographs, music, and other publications of every nature whatever, deposited in the said clerk's office, and not heretofore sent to the Department of the Interior, at Washington, together with all records of copyright in his possession, including the titles so recorded, and the dates of record: *Provided*, That where there are duplicate copies of legal, scientific, or mechanical works, one copy of each may be deposited in the library of the Patent Office, for which a receipt shall be given by the Commissioner of Patents to the Librarian of Congress.

Repealing Clause and Schedule.

Sec. 111. *And be it further enacted,* That the acts and parts of acts set forth in the schedule of acts cited, hereto annexed, are hereby repealed, without reviving any acts or parts of acts repealed by any of said acts, or by any clause or provisions therein: *Provided, however,* That the repeal hereby enacted shall not affect, impair, or take away any right existing under any of said laws; but all actions and causes of action, both in law and in equity, which have arisen under any of said laws, may be commenced and prosecuted and if already commenced may be prosecuted, to final judgment and execution, in the same manner as though this act had not been passed, excepting that the remedial provisions of this act shall be applicable to all suits and proceedings hereafter commenced; *And provided also,* That all applications for patents pending at the time of the passage of this act, in cases where the duty has been paid, shall be proceeded with and acted on in the same manner as though filed after the passage thereof: *And provided further,* That all offences which are defined and punishable under any of said acts, and all penalties and forfeitures created thereby, and incurred before this act takes effect, may be prosecuted, sued for, and recovered, and such offences punished according to the provisions of said acts, which are continued in force for such purpose.

Schedule of statutes cited and repealed, as printed in the Statutes at Large, including such portions only of the appropriation bills referred to as are applicable to the Patent Office.

Patents.

Act of July 4th, 1836, chap. 357, vol. 5, p. 117.
March 3d, 1837, chap. 45, vol. 5, p. 191.
March 3d, 1839, chap. 88, vol. 5, p. 353.
August 29th, 1842, chap. 263, vol. 5, p. 543.
August 6th, 1846, chap. 90, vol. 9, p. 59.
May 27th, 1848, chap. 47, vol. 9, p. 231.
March 3d, 1849, chap. 108, vol. 9, p. 395.
March 3d, 1851, chap. 32, vol. 9, p. 617.

Act of August 30th, 1852, chap. 107, vol. 10, p. 75.
August 31st, 1852, chap. 108, vol. 10, p. 76.
March 3d, 1853, chap. 97, vol. 10, p. 209.
April 22d, 1854, chap. 52, vol. 10, p. 276.
March 3d, 1855, chap. 175, vol. 10, p. 643.
August 18th, 1856, chap. 129, vol. 11, p. 81.
March 3d, 1859, chap. 80, vol. 11, p. 410.
February 18th, 1861, chap. 37, vol. 12, p. 130.
March 2d, 1861, chap. 88, vol. 12, p. 246.
March 3d, 1863, chap. 102, vol. 12, p. 796.
June 25th, 1864, chap. 159, vol. 13, p. 194.
March 3d, 1865, chap. 112, vol. 13, p. 533.
June 27th, 1866, chap. 143, vol. 14, p. 76.
March 29th, 1867, chap. 17, vol. 15, p. 10.
July 20th, 1868, chap. 177, vol. 15, p. 119.
July 23d, 1868, chap. 227, vol. 15, p. 168.
March 3d, 1869, chap. 121, vol. 15, p. 293

COPYRIGHTS.

Act of February 15th, 1819, chap. 19, vol. 3, p. 481.
February 3d, 1831, chap. 16, vol. 4, p. 436.
June 30th, 1834, chap. 157, vol. 4, p. 728.
August 18th, 1856, chap. 169, vol. 11, p. 138.
February 5th, 1859, chap. 22, vol. 11, p. 380.
February 18th, 1861, chap. 37, vol. 12, p. 130.
March 3d, 1865, chap. 126, vol. 13, p. 540.
February 18th, 1867, chap. 43, vol. 14, p. 395.

Approved July 8th, 1870.

NOTE.—The following is the text of the supplemental act relating to patents, approved March 3, 1871:

Be it enacted by the Senate and House of Representatives of the United States of America, in Congress assembled, That that part of section thirty-three of an act entitled "An act to revise, consolidate, and amend the statutes relating to patents and copyrights," approved July eight, eighteen hundred and seventy, which requires that, in case of application by assignee or assignees for reissue of letters-patent, the application shall be made and the specification sworn to by the inventor or discoverer, if living, shall not be construed to apply to patents issued and assigned prior to July eight, eighteen hundred and seventy.

APPROVED, March 3, 1871.

INDEX

TO PATENT, TRADE MARK, AND COPYRIGHT LAWS.

	SECTION
Abandonment, by incomplete application, for two years,	32
Additional clerks, &c.,	3
Application, how made,	26–30
in case of forfeited patents,	35
rejected or withdrawn,	35
to be completed in two years,	32
made by inventor in case of assignment,	33
by executor or administrator,	34
Appeal to board of examiners-in-chief,	46
to Commissioner,	47
to Supreme Court of District of Columbia,	48
mode of proceeding,	49, 50, 51
to Supreme Court of United States,	56
Assignees, patents or reissues to,	33
Assignments,	36
must be recorded within three months,	36
Assistant Commissioner how appointed,	2
salary,	4
to act in absence of Commissioner,	11
Bill in equity,	52
Bond, Commissioner and chief clerk,	6
Caveat, who may file,	40
certified copies of records to be evidence,	57
Circuit Courts to take cognizance of cases under patent laws,	55
Clerks,	2, 4
Copyists,	4
Commissioner, how appointed,	2
salary,	4
duties,	7
to give bond,	6
franking privilege,	8
report to Congress,	9
to make rules and regulations,	19
to establish rules for taking testimony,	43
appeal to,	47
to make rules, &c., regulating transfer of trade-marks,	81

	SECTION
Copyright, ...	85–110
Librarian of Congress to have charge of, . . .	85
who may obtain, and for what, ...	86
duration, ...	87
extension, ...	88
assignment, ...	89
requisites for obtaining, ...	90
two copies to be sent to Librarian of Congress, . .	90, 93
form of record and certificate, ...	91
fees for recording, &c., ...	92
copies of new editions to be sent, . . .	93
penalty for failure to deposit, ...	94
copyright matter free of postage, . . .	95
postmaster to give receipt, ...	96
form to be entered in or on copyright book, &c., . .	97
penalty for wrongly announcing that copyright has been obtained, ...	98
remedy for infringement, ...	99
penalty for substantial infringement of maps, designs, &c., ...	100
performance of dramatic compositions, . . .	101
publishing manuscript without consent, . . .	102
not applicable to foreigners or non-residents, . .	103
no action maintained unless within two years, . .	104
plea, ...	105
Circuit Courts to take cognizance, ...	106
appeal to Supreme Court, ...	107
costs in suits, ...	108
transfer to Librarian of Congress, ...	109
clerks to send matter now in hand to Librarian of Congress, ...	110
repealing clause, ...	111
Designs, ...	71–76
when models may be dispensed with, ...	72
duration, ...	73
extension, ...	74
fees, ...	75
Disbursements made by disbursing clerk of Interior Department, ...	69
Disclaimer, ...	54
to be made before suit, ...	60
Drawings in applications, ...	27
Examination, ...	31

	SECTION
Examiner in charge of interferences,	2
salary,	4
duty,	42
Examiners, principal,	2
salary,	4
first assistant,	2, 4
second assistant,	2, 4
Examiners-in-chief, how appointed,	2
salary,	4
duties,	10
appeal to,	46
Extension,	63–67
Fees,	68
how paid,	69
Final fee—if not paid within six months, patent withheld,	23
Foreign patent—effect on application in the United States,	25
to give date to American patent,	25
Franking privilege,	7
Infringement,	55
damages for,	59
plea and special matters to be proved,	61
Injunction,	55
Interferences,	42
Interfering applications,	42
Patents,	58
Laborers and watchmen,	4
Librarian,	2, 4
Library,	15
Machinist,	2, 4
Messenger and purchasing clerk,	2, 4
Models to be arranged and open to inspection,	13
in applications,	29
of rejected applications may be disposed of,	14
of designs,	72
Money received paid into treasury,	69
to be paid back,	70
Oath by administrator or executor applying,	34
of applicant, before whom to be taken,	30
of office,	5
Officers' and employees' oath,	5
not to acquire interest in patents,	16
Papers filed, when they may be printed,	18

	SECTION
Patent Office,	1
officers,	2
agents not recognized for misconduct,	17
Patents, date of,	23
for what granted,	24
withheld if final fee is not paid within six months,	23
what must contain,	22
how to be signed and recorded,	21
foreign,	25
forfeited application for renewal of,	35
"Patented" to be marked on articles,	38
erroneously marked,	39
Plea and special matters to be proved in suit for infringement,	61
Printing specifications, claims, decisions, &c.,	20
of illegible papers,	18
Re-examination of a rejected case,	41
Reissue,	53
Rejected and withdrawn applications, renewal of,	35
Repealing clause,	111
Report to Congress,	9
Rules and regulations,	19
for taking testimony, Commissioner to establish,	43
Salaries,	4
Seal,	12
Specimens in applications,	28
Subpœna issued by clerks of United States courts,	44
Sup. Ct. of Dist. of Col., appeal to and mode of proceeding,	48–51
Supreme Court of United States, writ of error or appeal to,	56
Trade-marks,	77–84
who may obtain protection for, and how,	77
duration, extent of protection, and extension,	78
remedy for infringement,	79
not a name alone,	79
what may be refused,	79
certified copy of mark and record to be evidence,	80
Commissioner to make rules and regulate transfer,	81
fraud in procuring registry,	82
act not to affect existing remedy,	83
no action to be maintained for fraudulent or improper,	84
Use in a foreign country if not patented or published,	62
of patentable article before patent,	37
Witnesses in cases pending in Patent Office,	45

www.ingramcontent.com/pod-product-compliance
Lightning Source LLC
Chambersburg PA
CBHW030404170426
43202CB00010B/1486